"In *The Polarized Mind*, Ki humanistic-depth-psychologic pervasive murderous plague arising from the human condition itself—*psychological polarization*, the elevation of one absolutist point of view to the exclusion, even demonization, of all others. Such polarization, Schneider shows, is the age-old antidote to the existential anxiety and panic evoked by the groundlessness, the nullity and finiteness, and the mystery and paradox of human existence, with which we are invariably confronted when we become subject to individual and collective trauma. Schneider deftly chronicles the destructive ideologies and power structures—forms of defensive grandiosity—through which human beings of various cultures and historical epochs have sought to evade and deny the groundlessness and mystery of their existence. Then he proposes what he calls an *awe-based reformation*, based on accepting and embracing the mystery of our being. Again drawing on examples from different cultures and historical periods, he offers radical and impressive proposals for the raising of "awe-grounded kids" and for creating a social order based more on awe than on existential panic. This book is an enormously important contribution not only to clinical psychology but to social and political psychology and philosophy as well. Written in reader-friendly language, it will be of great appeal to students, trainees, practitioners, and academics in all of these fields, as well as to educated readers concerned about the perils of human life in the 21st century."

-- Robert D. Stolorow, PhD, Author of *World, Affectivity, Trauma: Heidegger and Post-Cartesian Psychoanalysis*

"*The Polarized Mind is* excellent. In my estimation it is a 21st century extension of Rollo May's *Cry for Myth*. I mean this as the highest compliment."

--Sheldon Solomon, PhD, Social Psychologist, Skidmore College, co-founder of Terror Management Theory, and co-author of *In the Wake of 9/11*

"Erudite, eloquent, and elegant! This book connects the psychology of the polarizing mind with historical events that shaped the course of humanity through millennia. This excellent

volume illuminates social and cultural dynamics that are as relevant and dangerous today as they were ages ago."
-- Isaac Prilleltensky, PhD, Dean, School of Education, University of Miami, Author of *Promoting Well-Being*

"*The Polarized Mind* is, in my estimate, a logical extension, and deepened development of Schneider's previous ground-breaking book, *The Paradoxical Self*. In *The Polarized Mind*, Schneider mounts a penetrating analysis of the 'sickness unto death' (Kierkegaard) resulting from the 'either/or' rigidity in contemporary political, corporate, cultural, religious and healing arenas. Schneider denies he is issuing a 'utopian manifesto,' but comes close to doing just that in a sober clarion call for weighing the liberating potential of integrative thinking in contrast to the destructive power of dichotomous thinking. As with Schneider's previous writings, this is a hard one to put down."
--Benjamin R. Tong, PhD, Professor, Clinical Psychology Psy.D. Program, California Institute of Integral Studies, San Francisco. Tai Ch'i, QiGong & Taoist studies instructor. Emeritus faculty, Asian American Studies Department, San Francisco State University. Psychotherapist and organizational consultant in private practice

"*The Polarized Mind* is not only very timely, it is also very moving. It certainly had a big impact on me not only during my waking hours when I tossed the book's thought-provoking ideas consciously around in my head but also while sleeping, in my dreams. I, like many people in these troubled times, have been searching for answers to what we are facing and *The Polarized Mind* comes as a deeply revealing source of alternatives. For example, I embrace the book's recommendations for following wisdom traditions that stress a fluid center of belief, humility and adventurousness as the paths to balance and fulfillment. I also find it encouraging to note that the world has had leadership examples like Gandhi and Washington to serve as role models for this path."
-- Sonja Saltman, PhD, co-founder of the Saltman Center for Conflict Resolution at the University of Nevada at Las Vegas (UNLV) Boyd School of Law

THE POLARIZED MIND
WHY IT'S KILLING US
AND WHAT WE CAN DO ABOUT
IT

By
Kirk J. Schneider, PhD

University Professors Press
Colorado Springs, CO

First Published in 2013, University Professors Press

ISBN-13: 978-1-939686-00-8

University Professors Press
Colorado Springs, CO

Cover Design by Laura Ross, 2013

Contents

Acknowledgments

I am indebted to Godella von Kirschbach and Scott Gibbs for their tireless and illuminating early feedback on this volume. Equally important, I am deeply appreciative of their belief in me and in the cause of this work. I am also indebted to my wife, Jurate, without whose red pen this manuscript would feel very blue.

Finally, I would like to acknowledge Louis Hoffman and Shawn Rubin, chief editors (and founders) of University Professors Press. I am so pleased to accompany them on this initial, radically humanizing foray into publishing.

Foreword

The Polarized Mind is one of the great reflections on humanity. It is a wide-ranging mix of history, politics, philosophy, anthropology, and psychology/psychotherapy based on an incredible amount of knowledge and scientific facts. Above all, *The Polarized Mind* is a peak of existential-humanistic inquiry and of what it is capable of producing.

This is the mature book by an extremely sensitive and respectful psychologist whose expertise gives him the capacity to look in depth at the human psyche, which is doubtless behind all political, economic, social, and individual behavior. While Schneider is able to interconnect the great changes, cycles, and polarizations throughout history with human nature and psychodynamic defense mechanisms, he also discovered a deeper cause according to recent research—the existential fear of groundlessness—and thus shows the root of a danger which he calls the plague of our time.

This is an existential analysis of our historical and actual situation. But it is also a guidebook for a better future, showing the way out of this urgent and dangerous collective situation by underscoring what is possible through personal growth. Personal growth is Schneider's antidote to the tendencies of our time toward quick fix solutions, which again lead to more polarization and groupings.

The Polarized Mind, finally, is written in an artistic style. It is a pleasure to step with the author through history and science, to see how changes in history are connected with psychology and how both interact, to see the philosophy behind historical movements and to understand better the interconnections of all through the phenomenological testimonies of those who lived them.

This is a wise book—wise because of the deep understanding of what it means to be human and because of its reconciling spirit which brings together the brutality of human one-sidedness with the equally human love for life and for the person.

--Alfried Längle, MD, President of the International Society for Logotherapy and Existential Analysis, Vienna, Austria

Preface

The polarized mind, which is the fixation on one point of view to the utter exclusion of competing points of view, is killing us—and has been for millennia. Sometimes it is killing us blatantly, such as in the recent spate of mass shootings at public gatherings or the preemptive wars initiated by myopic rulers; and sometimes it is killing us insidiously, such as in the recent string of banking scandals, or the corporatization of politics, or the splintering of ethnicities.

While there have been increasing discussions of the polarized mind—from the classic research of authoritarian personality by Adorno and colleagues (1950), to the obedience studies of Milgram (1962) to the treatises on "opposable minds" (Martin, 2009), "divided minds" (Sunstein, (2011), and "righteous minds" (Haidt, 2012)—few have drawn from the intimate observations of depth or existential inquiry.[1] Further, few have proposed existentially or spiritually informed alternatives to the polarized conditions under which we labor, such as the "awe-based" vision that I propose in this volume.

This book, then, is an attempt to redress the gap in our understanding—as well as treatment—of polarized minds. In this book, I will detail the nature of the polarization problem, the history of its consequences, and the imperative alternatives available to redress it. For example, in the first part of the book, I detail how upheavals in the histories of cultures can parallel traumas in the histories of their leaders, which in turn can lead to polarized, tyrannical rule. In the second part of the book, I show

---

[1] Adorno and colleagues' study of the authoritarian personality, like Milgram's classic study of obedience several years later, focused mainly on laboratory investigations of authoritarian personality and its cultural and socioeconomic context. Sunstein's study highlighted social psychological evidence for extreme behavior, and Martin's investigation emphasized a cognitive approach to integrative vs. dichotomous thinking. Haidt, finally, took an evolutionary perspective on political and religious rigidity (or "righteousness") based on group needs for adaptation and survival. While each of these studies is highly illuminating within its own sphere, none seem to me to address the bigger questions about how trauma, existential anxiety, and sense of significance impact polarized—as well as comparatively nonpolarized—experiential states.

how the cultivation of the sense of awe—that is, humility and wonder—toward living can be an antidote to polarization. Specifically, I show how the sense of awe is the basis for many of the great wisdom traditions throughout history—frequently the very same cultures I depict earlier as polarized. Further, I show that if we are to have a chance at lasting change, these wisdom traditions can—and indeed *need to*—impact every major level of our lives. These levels include but are not exhausted by childrearing practices, the educational system, the work setting, and governance.

This book, finally, is not a utopian manifesto. It does not offer ultimate resolution. However, what it does offer is my vantage point as a depth psychologist. In this role, I have tended to many polarized lives, including my own, and witnessed remarkable life-transitions. Can our society, and indeed world, make similar transitions? I believe so, and there is no greater urgency.

Kirk J. Schneider

Introduction

*The fanatic is perpetually incomplete and insecure. He cannot
generate self-assurance...but finds it only by clinging
passionately to whatever support he happens to embrace.*
Eric Hoffer (1951)

*What man really fears is not so much extinction,
but extinction without significance.*
Ernest Becker (1975)

This book is about a murderous plague. There is nothing new
about this plague; it has been with us since the dawn of
humanity. However, what is new is its capacity to demolish:
both ourselves and our planet. What is also new is that thanks to
psychological depth research,[2] we now have a handle on this
plague's nature: it is confined neither to cultures nor individuals,
minorities nor majorities, but embraces the entirety of humanity.
The plague to which I refer is psychological *polarization.*

Psychological polarization is the elevation of one point of
view to the utter exclusion of competing points of view. It is
akin to but also differs from extremism. It is akin to extremism
in that it is of a "character or kind farthest removed from the
ordinary or average" (Random House, 1968, p. 470), but it is
distinguished from extremism in its emphasis on opposition as
much or more than advocacy. Whereas extremism can be based
on a variety of motivations, polarization tends to be based on
one: fear. When one is polarized, one tends to be panicked at
some level and the valence or intensity is around avoidance of

---

[2] By "psychological depth research," I mean *existentially informed* quantitative
and qualitative analyses of the human condition. These analyses include the
insights of existential psychology, anthropology, and philosophy;
psychoanalytic and analytical psychology; and critical philosophy.   In
particular, psychological depth research addresses the basic conditions of
human life, such as our smallness (fragility, limits) as well as greatness
(resiliency, freedom) before existence; and it considers the implications of
these conditions for personal and collective well-being.   For an excellent
contemporary overview of psychological depth research, see Shaver &
Mikulincer (2012a).

contrasting points of view. Polarization has also been called "black-and-white thinking," over-identification, and idol worship; but it was Paul Tillich (1963a), one the great theologians of the twentieth century, who probably put it best. Polarization, he said, in effect is demonization—the mistaking of a piece of reality for its entirety, or a part for the whole (p.140).

In this book, I will show how polarization kills, both literally and figuratively. Furthermore, I will show how polarization is more than just the extremism or fanaticism of a few, but a pervasive malady of twenty-first century life. It is evident, for example, in our dietary habits as well as our occupation with drugs; our political stands as well as our enthrallment with weaponry; our religious decrees as well as our adoration of technology; our shopping patterns as well as our fixation on fame; and our depression rates, as well as our obsession with efficiency. It is also evident in our personal and collective swings of mood, leading to a seemingly endless cycle of wider and deeper swings.

Put somewhat differently, I will show that the core problem with polarization is not so much in isolated behaviors, but in polarization *itself.* This is a great underappreciated problem because so often throughout history we focus on extreme acts— such as a mass shooting, or a preemptive war, or a belligerent crowd—but not the disposition that gave rise to them. And to lose sight of that underlying disposition is to miss the core problem: why polarizations occur so frequently in our own and other cultures, and how best to prevent them, which is the focus of the second half of this work.

In sum, polarization is a life-long contemporary problem. One type of polarization can lead to or replace another, and most types of polarization seem to derive from a singular psychospiritual source. Next, we will look at the nature of this source and how it can generate such destruction, both for individuals and for groups.

PART 1

WHY POLARIZATION IS KILLING US

Consider the following kaleidoscope of recent twentieth and twenty-first century events. What could they possibly have in common?

1933–1939. Adolph Hitler declares the thousand-year Reich, rallies millions in cities like Nuremberg and Berlin, and initiates the mass annihilation of Jews, Gypsies, and all those considered mentally defective.

1937. The Japanese imperial army savagely attacks mainland China—slaughters up to a quarter of a million Chinese noncombatants in Nanking in less than two months.

1951–1954. Senator Joseph McCarthy organizes the House Committee on Un-American Activity to prosecute "communist infiltration" among the ranks of some of the most distinguished writers and artists of the twentieth century.

1953–1973. The U.S. government, with the backing of major multinational corporations, supports the overthrow of elected leaders from Mohammed Massadegh in Iran to Salvador Allende in Chile to establish a free market, U.S.-style hegemony.

1967. Mao Zedong unleashes a "cultural revolution" in China; intellectual dissent is decimated.

1956–1968. Soviet troops crush anti-communist, pro-freedom uprisings in Hungary and Czechoslovakia.

1967–1972. Following its victory in the six-day war, the Israeli government takes the fateful step of annexing territory beyond its established border with Palestine. An elite force of Palestinian terrorists slaughters 12 Israeli Olympic athletes.

1966–1970. Counter-cultural gurus such as Timothy Leary advise young people to "turn on, tune in, and drop out." Supermodels like Twiggy popularize a malnourished look suggestive of anorexia.

1995. A single follower of an anti-government militia movement blows up a federal building in the American Midwest.

2001. Nineteen men organized under the banner of Islamic Fundamentalism commandeer two jetliners and ram them into the twin towers of the World Trade Center in New York City.

2002. President George W. Bush declares Iran, North Korea, and Iraq the "axes of evil" and sets the course for a preemptive war on Iraq.

Fifty-nine percent of the U.S. population believes that the prophesies in the Book of Revelations (such as the Rapture and a war with Islam in the final reckoning) will come true, and nearly a quarter believe that the Bible predicted the 9/11/2001 attacks.

2004–2005. Over 10 million U.S. children are prescribed anti-depressant drugs. Global warming and obesity reach pandemic proportions.

2008. Zealous over-speculation cripples world markets.

2010. The U.S. Supreme Court rules that corporations may make unlimited contributions to political campaigns.

2011. Calling the killings "cruel" but "necessary," Neo-Nazi Anders Behring Breivik slaughters 93 people at a Norwegian resort.

2012. "Honor killing" in parts of the Middle East is estimated to take the life of one woman a day.

2013. In the month following the Newtown massacre in which 20 elementary school students and 6 adults lost their lives, there were 900 gun deaths in the United States.

What do all these scenarios have in common? They all share two outstanding traits: They all represent forms and degrees of polarization (e.g., fixations on one set of values to the utter exclusion of other sets of values), and they all emerged as reactions against previous polarizations, as we shall see later in this volume, spiraling down through history. The scenarios share one more commonality: They've decimated countless lives. Given the weight of this outcome, it is incumbent on us to study it further. It is incumbent on us to study the worldwide pandemic of polarization; for it is through excavation that we may discover emancipation.

The Bases of Polarization

Throughout human history, people have repeatedly swung between extremes. Arthur Schlesinger Jr. (1986) noted these swings in his classic book *The Cycles of American History.* In this book, Schlesinger articulated the continuous political swings in U.S. history, particularly those between conservatism and liberalism, rigidity and permissiveness. But, as the examples above illustrate, there are many other forms of such swings in many other times and places.

The usual explanations for the swings of history, as well as individuals, are cultural, political, and biological. The founders of the United States swung away from the British motherland because of political and religious oppression. Certain nineteenth century abolitionists resorted to armed struggle because of unrelenting federal support of slavery. Post World War I Germany amassed a titanic arsenal, in part to avenge the humiliation it perceived at the Treaty of Versailles. McCarthyite anti-communists swelled in number following the advent of Soviet expansionism in Eastern Europe. And so on. Schlesinger provides a cogent summation of these various dynamics:

> The roots of...cyclical self-sufficiency doubtless lie deep in the natural life of humanity. There is a cyclical pattern in organic nature—in the tides, in the seasons, in the night and

day, in the systole and diastole of the human heart....People
can never be fulfilled for long either in the public or in the
private sector. We try one, then the other, and frustration
compels a change in course. Moreover, however effective a
particular course may be in meeting one set of troubles, it
generally falters and fails when new troubles arise. (pp.
27–28)

At the individual level, too, the conventional wisdom
embraces both cultural and biological explanations. Depression
is now frequently considered a biologically based disorder,
rooted in an imbalance of Serotonin in the brain. Anorexia, too,
is often considered a biologically and culturally based condition,
stemming from an overemphasis on thinness in Western
fashions. Obsessive-compulsiveness, mania, criminality, and
many other forms of suffering are also considered combinations
of biologically or genetically based chemical imbalances and
familial or cultural influences.

However, thanks to the expanding insights of psychological
depth research, we now have a clearer picture that what we once
took to be biologically or culturally based appears to be rooted in
a much thornier problem—the condition of being human. What
I mean by this is that polarization in all forms appears to be
based not just on a reaction against a particular family, or
society, or physiology but on the shocking nature of the human
condition itself, which, at its extremes, is the most daunting
condition of all.

And what is this human condition (or "condition humane,"
as Andre Malreaux put it)? It is the relationship of the human
being to the groundlessness of space and time, to death, and to
the most radical mystery of all, existence itself.

Just consider, for example, what happens in a classic pattern
of polarization. A person or persons become injured, and the
injury leads to a reaction. This reaction might take the form of a
religious decree to rid the world of infidels (e.g., those who had
formerly attempted to undermine established religious
precepts). It might take the form of a political mobilization
(e.g., fanatical nationalism) in the wake of a threatened state
(e.g., post World War I Germany). Or it might take the form of
a humiliated individual vowing to avenge his abusers. In each of

these cases there is a time-tested dynamic at play. Initially there is a sense of helplessness (despair), then there is a reaction against that helplessness (polarization, fanaticism), followed by a destructive outbreak as a result of that reaction.

Hence, if we peel back the layers of this scenario, what do we find? We certainly find physiological (e.g., fight and flight) reactions (as Schlesinger and others have noted), classical psychodynamic issues stemming from childhood (as Freud and others have contended), and behavioral dimensions, such as conditioned reactions to aversive stimuli (as Skinner and others have pointed out). But are these really the essential building blocks of polarized experiences, of stuck and life-encompassing fixations, or the extremes and fanaticisms of theocracies, military-industrial complexes, and hate-driven assassins? The emerging consensus is quite probably "no."

Although the traditional explanations work to a point, depth research unveils that they are but harbingers or glimpses of a much more encompassing problem. For example, the latest research on the roots of extremism centers on what is aptly termed "terror management theory" (see Pyszczynski, Solomon, & Greenberg, 2003; Greenberg, Koole, & Pyszczynski, 2004). In this theory, built on a growing base of cross-cultural research, the deeper we probe the layers of psychosocial extremes, the closer we come to anxieties about existence itself—coinciding with and extending beyond the physiological, familial, and cultural. In short, according to Terror Management Theory, polarization arises from culturally diversified experiences of death anxiety, and death anxiety is aroused by an extraordinary range of secondary fears.[3] Among these fears is humiliation, or

---

[3] Psychodynamic theorists such as Firestone & Catlett (2009), Fromm (1965), Laing (1969), Kohut (1977), Miller (2009), Stolorow (2011), and Yalom (1980) have shown that death anxiety (or what Kohut [1977, pp. 102–104] has aptly termed "disintegration anxiety") can be triggered by many developmental stressors including physical and emotional abuse, neglect, abandonment, humiliation, shaming, and depersonalization. That which the cognitive psychologists (e.g., Beck, 1976) call catastrophic thinking is also an example of the volatility of traumatized experience. Catastrophic thinking is based on catastrophic fears, and catastrophic fears are inexorably associated with death, groundlessness, and the break-up of the self (see also Grottstein, 1990 and Eigen, 1993).

the terror of feeling *insignificant.* Witness the following conclusion by Arie Kruglanski, one of the leading investigators of global terrorism. Drawing in part on Terror Management research, and in part on the data that he and his colleagues at the National Consortium for the Study of Terrorism and Responses to Terrorism have amassed, he asserts:

> Personal significance is a motivation that has been recognized by psychological theorists as a major driving force of human behavior. Terrorists feel that through suicide, their lives will achieve tremendous significance. They will become heroes, martyrs. In many cases, their decision is a response to great loss of significance, which can occur through humiliation, discrimination or personal problems...Interesting[ly], research shows that poverty is not the root cause of terrorism. Many terrorists come out of the middle class, and some [like Osama Bin Laden] are quite well-to-do. (cited in Jacobs, 2010, pp. 36–39)

As Kruglanski intimates, therefore, terrorism in particular and polarization in general are rooted in a very profound problem of the human situation. It is not a problem that can simply be eliminated through material comforts, physical well-being, or even in some cases loving and well-adjusted families. It is a problem that each individual must confront in varying degrees during their lifetimes, because it is not a problem that will go away. Although physical and psychological vulnerability and ultimately annihilation appear to be at the crux of this problem, I suggest that there is something even more subtle at play, something even more harrowing. This "something" is what I and others call "existential anxiety." Existential anxiety is not just the fear of physical death but the fear of the implications of physical death. Existing in a universe that has no calculable end and no calculable beginning—that is a radical mystery. It is our terror of our bewildering fragility, our nothingness before the vastness of space and time, and our steady transformation from matter to inexplicable dust (see also Kruglanski, Gelfand, & Gunaratna, 2012; Schneider, 1999).

Trauma, shock, and disruption all signal us to this incomprehensible state of affairs. They jar us out of our comfort zones and peel back the profundities lying just beneath our routines. Virtually everyone who is polarized, I contend, has been a victim of existential panic; and virtually all of us, in varying degrees, have experienced this polarization. The question is: How do we prevent, or at least manage, the most destructive polarizations—the polarizations that wage egregious wars, that initiate relentless hatred, that concentrate obscene accumulation of wealth, and that deplete, everyday, the imperative resources of nations?

Before we can address this question, we need to look more thoroughly at the psychological bases of polarization throughout history, the damage that polarization has wreaked, and the fates that have awaited those who fought valiantly to oppose it.

Chapter 1

The Denial of Mystery Through History

Except for some radiant departures, human history is strewn with the casualties of one-sidedness. Rarely in the annals of civilization have people prioritized *mystery* as the cornerstone of their vitality; and yet the wisest among them have foretold differently.

From the time of the Babylonian cuneiform, people have striven for answers; they need to know if a god is watching over them, or a storm can be weathered, or a plant can be harvested and so on. Yet answers are very much double-edged swords. On the one hand they guide and manage, but on the other they imprison, keep us from venturing, and prejudice us against competing "answers" that may prove superior. Hence, the problem is not answers per se. It is the attachment to certain kinds of answers—the attachment to all-pervading "truths"—that get us into trouble. And it is remarkable how much trouble this one simple problem, this polarizing mentality, arouses.

Over and over again cultures repeat the problem to which I refer. We never seem to learn. Just consider the formation of religious dogma. We started out scared and vulnerable in this world and created simple deities to assuage our terrors; then we developed entire empires based on the defense of our simple guardians. Think of the "progression" from Neolithic cults to official state religions and from tribal councils to vast national institutions—such as the priesthood of ancient Egypt, the assemblies of Rome, the papacy of early Christianity, and the caliphate of traditional Islam. And think of the blood, not to mention intellectual capital that was drained by these behemoth power centers. Consider the prejudice, hatred, and dehumanization spread by their absolutism: the slaughter of dissidents, the humiliation of outsiders, the sacrifice of innocents, and the squelching of intellects. Think of the

succession of ever-intensifying polarizations and blood feuds
that have resulted—from the epic battles between the
Babylonians and the Assyrians, the Jews and the Philistines, the
Greeks and the Persians, the Romans and the Goths, the
Christians and the Moslems, the Hindus and the Moslems, the
Chinese and the Mongols, the Turks and the Huns, and the
British and the French, to name just a *few*!

No matter where we look in the ancient—or for that matter,
modern—world, we find mystery-phobic power structures,
whether they take the form of religious institutions or
monarchies, belief systems or militia.   Wherever there was
dogma, there was fear; and wherever there was certainty there
was insecurity.   These qualities ran rampant not only through
rich and imperial oligarchies such as the church, the priesthood,
the government, and the academy, but also at the micro-level via
folkways and local myths.   Indeed, an entire web of polarizing
fantasies seized the many and diverse populations of the world.
These fantasies ran from the sovereignty and absolute authority
of the father to the compulsion to be a "good boy" or "good girl"
lest a deity would exact revenge; and from rumors about
foreigners to bigotries about people who deviate from the norm.

At the risk of over-dramatizing the problem of polarization, I
readily acknowledge that there were notable exceptions to the
examples that I have thus far portrayed.   There were palpable
pockets of freedom, for example, to perceive or discover one's
life anew.   Absolutist beliefs were not omnipresent, and there
certainly were occasions for which such "disturbing" events as
the passage of the stars, or the charisma of a stranger, or the
ecstasy of carnal pleasure were reconsidered. However, it is sad
to say that in my view, and the view of many of who have
rigorously   investigated   the   matter,   these   pockets   of
reconsideration were more the exception than the rule, and war
or devaluation were (and continue to be) the order of the times.

Hence, it is my thesis here that human beings have
frequently lived not unlike terrorized rats trapped in a cage.
Curiously, we have turned away from our awesome predicament
and toward some kind of fantasized salvation, leaping, scurrying,
and devouring in our fruitless quest.   We have even woven
compelling tales about how we have faced the challenges of our

daunting condition, either through our gods, our militaries, our rulers, our adornments, our progeny, our ethnicity, or our nationalities (to name but a sample!). But rarely have we admitted to ourselves how inadequate these contrivances have been, and how generally despairing! For to do so would mean admitting that we mostly resort to half-measures in the development of our lives. Even more dispiriting, it would mean the subversion of tremendous vested interests in this charade, such as those extracted by blood, capital, or greed. To do so, moreover, would expose whole systems as the pale and over-bloated substitutes that they are. Consider here, for example, the "glamour" of wealth, or the "glory" of war, or the "greatness" of one's religion, nationality, or race or, for that matter, town, village or sports team! To be sure, wealth and even war have attractive elements; religion, ethnic origins, and even sports teams can have marvelous dimensions. But as be-alls and end-alls, alphas and omegas? Come on. That's killing us. That's taking this incredible inexplicable recipe that is humanity, squeezing all the nutrients out of it, and mashing it into one paltry vessel. How about all the other vessels out there? How about all the other openings to life?

This whole problem, of course, amounts to a vicarious life, a life lived not particularly for oneself but through other powers, as the esteemed cultural anthropologist Ernest Becker (1973) put it. It's a way to cope with the terror and beauty of existence but at a devastating price—one's aliveness. Yet the vicarious life is extremely seductive apparently, because it has been time tested throughout history.

The Groundlessness Problem

The question arises, then: Why, historically, have we settled for second-rate lives? Why have we poured our energy and talent into war machines, national identities, and culturally created gods? Don't we have anything better to do with our own lives? Isn't the amazement and passion we seek in others—be they people or things—dormant within ourselves? I think so, but more about that later. Right now, the issue is the long history of mystery *denial* and what perpetuates it.

To answer this question, we need to start with what we proposed earlier: Polarization begins with fear, and extreme polarization begins with extreme fear. Extreme fear, depth research has revealed, associates not just with loss of values or even loss of life; but with complete loss of orientation—in a word, *groundlessness*. The sense of groundlessness, in turn, leads to great defensive maneuvers to regain ground, or *significance.*—and not just ordinary ground or significance but enormous height (*glory*) to defy even a hint of the former vulnerability. Civilizations, like individuals, will do all they can to avoid associations to their helplessness before the cosmos, and much of what they do—generally at their own and others' peril—is to create the illusion that they are equal to the cosmos (Becker, 1973; Hoffer, 1951). This pretension to omnipotence, as I term it, is evident in civilizations from ancient Egypt to imperial Rome and from Byzantium to colonial Europe, whose downfalls have been equally evident, based on the pretensions of their origins. Although these civilizations clearly had other motives besides defensive omnipotence, it is the defensive omnipotence that endangered them, and that led ultimately to their collapse.

Hence, what we have here is a cycle of fear (e.g., attack by foreign adversary), overcompensation for that fear through inflation of state authority, and subsequent demise of that authority through inability to fulfill its pretension. Think of Athens' decision to invade Sparta or Rome's presumption of global rule or Christendom's designs on Islam, or vice-versa, or the British rule of Southeast Asia or virtually any dominator state over any submitter state. A cycle proceeds where a formerly moderate or even submissive state is transformed into a dominator state through panic, and then implodes from its own inflated presumption. But the point here is not simply to anatomize the outward features of the polarization cycle. This is a fairly familiar story. The more relevant point for our purposes is to anatomize the inward, subtler features of the polarization cycle, which are just now becoming more perceptible. On this latter point, then, we need to look closely at the motives of polarized societies to give us in-depth clues both as to their destructiveness as well as possible redemption.

Pretensions to Omnipotence, Both Large and Small

One of the first clues we have about the *cosmic* stakes of polarization are the lengths to which cultures will go to maintain it. Consider, for example, the time and energy invested historically not just in equipping massive armies but in *adorning* them. Why isn't a sword or a canon enough? No, most great powers had to possess stylized swords or canons, gilded or bejeweled uniforms, colossal scepters or radiant amulets, dramatic insignias (e.g., crosses), and flashy military colors. It was not enough that armies simply did their duty; they had to "scream" with intimidating symbolism, thunder with patriotic pride, and dazzle with firepower. I think these displays are no mere accidents of warfare. The raging throngs assembled for Stalin's military parades, the frenzied masses at Hitler rallies, the fanfare at Roman war parades, the blaring trumpets, the pounding pulpits, the blazing banners—all these were designed to match, not just flirt with, cosmic predominance. These adornments, either wittingly or unwittingly, conspire to evoke infallibility, insurmountability, and deification. How else to explain the ornate, enveloping palaces; the towering statues of deities; the equally towering temples, churches, and state buildings; the coats of arms and the "Thousand Year Reichs"; the invincible "Soviet Man" and the unassailable "Operation Freedom"; the Brown shirts and the Black shirts; the fancy chariots and the gleaming Mercedes, and so on. Or how about the small-scale pretenses to omnipotence that we've seen every day on city and village streets, in farming communities, and in jungles? These run from the two-bit gangs who "own" their turf, to the mafia chieftains who oversee global drug operations, to the greed-obsessed bank presidents who speculate at will, to the schoolyard bullies who brutalize with abandon.

Diverse as they are, these desperately striving, immortality-fixated individuals and cultures can be understood on the basis of a comprehensive theory of development. This theory doesn't simply resort to fight or flight reactions or reductions to narcissistic wounding; it reaches beyond to a stark assessment of existential striving. Consider, for example, how what I term the paradox principle may be useful here (Schneider, 1999). The paradox principle has three basic tenets: One, human experience embraces a continuum from constriction to expansion. Constriction is understood is as the capacity to draw back and confine thoughts, feelings, and sensations, while expansion is the capacity to burst forth and extend thoughts, feelings, and sensations. Two, the more persons or cultures deny their paradoxical nature the more they become polarized; the more they become polarized (i.e., compelled) toward either constriction or expansion, the more they become destructive. Three, the more persons or cultures can face or choose their constrictive or expansive capacities, the more versatile they can become, and the more they can *respond* to rather than react against what a given situation demands.

Hence, if we apply this principle to polarized groups throughout history, some quite intriguing patterns emerge. One of the first patterns is that no matter how polarized people become in one direction (e.g., constrictive), they almost invariably also become polarized, at least partially, in the opposite direction (e.g., expansive). This dynamic played out in early Christendom, for example, when papal authority not only pressed people to *add* certain thoughts, feelings, and behaviors to their daily repertoire (e.g., devotion to Christ, church attendance), but also to *relinquish* other or competing thoughts, feelings, and behaviors (e.g., devotion to foreign gods, pagan practices). The combination here amounts to what we might term a double polarization. While the main polarization may be in the direction of expansionism and revolt against a previous order (e.g., Roman imperialism), the secondary polarization is in the direction of hyperconstriction, or extreme exclusivity of the prevailing order.

Why this seemingly contradictory state of affairs? To answer this question, we need to look more closely at the constrictive–expansive dynamic and its rootedness in ontological depth theory, to which we previously referred. Expansionist powers such as early institutional Christianity (or, for that matter, imperial Rome or dynastic Egypt) are motivated not only to defy anything that belittles or diminishes them but to embrace all that inflates them (to equate themselves with the universe). Yet this tack only carries such powers so far. At some point they begin to buckle under the weight of their ambitiousness; greatness becomes too much, and they need to draw back. As Becker (1973) has noted, no human powers can be straightforwardly expansive, lest they crack and eventually break up. This lesson is repeatedly suffered but rarely heeded, and the result is the very disaster that the inflated people seek tirelessly to avoid—impotency, smallness, and obliteration.

The idea that oppressor groups have only so much power, are vulnerable, and could potentially become overwhelmed dogs them incessantly. The last thing that inflated individuals or cultures need is to realize that they lack control. Therefore, to develop a bulwark against that potentiality and against the realization that they are not comparable to gods, oppressor groups develop elaborate fantasy systems of control. Ancient Rome, for example, forbade the worship of non-Roman gods; officers of the Spanish inquisition forced Christian piety; European royalty enslaved nonlanded workers, and the like. By the twentieth century, the hyperconstrictions of oppressor groups reached new depths of depravity. Consider the array of prohibitions within Nazi Germany—laws against race mixing, Jewish-owned businesses, inter-racial marriages, homosexuality, psychotherapy, liberal education, Jewish professors, schools, synagogues, mental retardates, gypsies, and non-Aryan citizenship. In Stalin's Russia, there were laws against private ownership and businesses, liberal education, non-communist political parties, and non-state-approved organizations. In imperial Japan, freedom of expression was squelched, citizenry sworn to complete loyalty to the emperor, and soldiers obliged to die in suicidal military operations. In Maoist China, intellectual dissent was crushed, books by foreign sources banned, artistic freedom thoroughly curtailed. In each of these countries, entire groups were forced into state-supported agendas, and soldiers were forced to march in lock step with one another, much like mechanical toys, completely devoid of personality. The degree of contradictoriness in such cultures that aspired to deific status was astounding, both in terms of pomposity and paralysis, ferocity and the most crippling type of reserve. Yet such contradictions failed to faze these cultures, as their fragilities were completely dismissed. It is incredible how easily they lived

with the fantasy of omnipotence when impotence abounded both
in their leaders and in the systems espoused. Yet in the end, of
course, it was the impotency that overwhelmed, and the great
task of rebuilding—removed of original presumptiveness—
began.

As we shall see, the bipolarity of polarization (e.g.,
dimensions of both hyperconstriction and hyperexpansion,
repression and aggression) were not confined to cultures that
dominated. Indeed, the terror of smallness and subsequent warp
into greatness (or what pretended to be greatness) infected a
variety of cultures both large and small. Nietzsche called this
problem *ressentiment* and attributed it mainly to cultures, such as
Christianity and Judaism, that arose from slavery, but it certainly
was not confined to these arenas (Kaufmann, 1968). Bipolarity
can also be seen in groups that start out and remain oppressed.
Indeed, consider all the oppressed groups throughout history that
found their own ways to compensate for their victimhood, either
through internal hierarchies or extravagant displays of pride.
Reflect, for example, on the varieties of self-aggrandizement
among oppressed religious minorities, calling themselves
"armies of God," or the "chosen people," or the "one true faith,"
and so on. Or consider all the oppressed groups who break up
into regional factions, such as in Somalia or inner-city America,
where one clan or leader is pitted against another or one clan or
leader rules an underground empire.

Finally, there is one question that remains: How can
individuals and groups who have *not* directly suffered the trauma
of their forebears remain committed to their forebears'
polarization, as we've seen in successive generations of racists,
fanatics, and imperialists down through history? Again, while
there are no simple answers here, what I have elsewhere called
vicarious or "implicit trauma" may be pertinent (Schneider,
1999). Implicit trauma is the subtle or hidden trauma that can be
passed down from generation to generation on the basis of covert
messages. Just as the battle-hardened father in a small family
can transmit messages of revulsion toward his war-time enemies,
an entire culture can transmit similar messages about another
entire culture to countless succeeding generations. These latter
generations do not have to witness even a fragment of what their

forebears experienced in order to carry out their obsessive designs; all it takes are the volatile combinations of convincing cultural stories (e.g., myths) and early, impressionable imprinting.

In sum, we must realize that a collective is an organism made up of individual organisms. As such the collective is subject to the same existential anxieties, the same maddening defensive maneuvers as the individual, albeit on a much grander and more destructive scale.

Testimonies: Mystery Denial from the Inside

While it is one thing, as previously intimated, to talk about polarizing societies, it is quite another to hear from them directly, through their own sentiments and words. In this spirit, then, let us explore presently some real-life illustrations of the denial of mystery throughout history. This inquiry will examine both the pivotal leadership of polarized movements, as well as the citizenry who followed them. We will confine ourselves to the historical power centers of the world (as defined by military as well as material might), because they pose the greatest challenge to our collective survival. We will also confine ourselves to the personal, political, and religious dimensions of these power centers, since they seem most integral to polarization. Our questions will be consistent throughout: How did people become so extreme? What formed their leaders' extremism, as well as the extremism of those who emulated them in the culture at large? What consequences resulted from such personal and collective fury? (Or to paraphrase the psychiatrist R.D. Laing [1967]: What has prompted hundreds of thousands of normal men to destroy hundreds of thousands of other normal men over the last hundred thousand years?)

Right from the outset, polarization has undergone a dizzying array of expressions. It has appeared as bigotry, bullying, tyranny, vengefulness, and arrogance; and it has also manifested as narrowness, rigidity, pedantry, and obsession. It can also be seen in fields as diverse as governance, religion, and science. Accompany me now as we explore the power of polarization through five millennia of leaders and followers who embraced it. My hope is that this excursion will help us grasp the impact of polarization not just on a given culture or era but on humanity as a whole. Although we all know something about extremist people throughout history, most of us know little, in my view, about the psychology of those people—in their own words, from their own hearts. Here, then, is a chance to explore that psychology and the foundational influence it has for our diverse and polarizing present.

One final note: The inquiry to follow is not intended to be exhaustive or historically detailed. It is intended to provide what I call "historical haiku," or snapshots of essential polarizing mentalities. Again, my focus in this book is on the psychological, or more accurately *psychospiritual*, bases for polarized mentalities; it is not on comprehensive historical detail.[4]

Babylon and the Birth of Polarized Minds

There is perhaps no better place to begin our testimonials then from one of the earliest parables known to humanity—the Babylonian text known as the *Enuma Elish* (circa 3500 B.C.E). In this prototypal document, the forces of chaos and order, groundlessness and stability clash to create the first polarizations of the newly created universe. The story begins with the following scenario: "When there was no heaven, no earth, no height, no depth, no name...when there were no gods," there were only the eternal, primordial beings Apsu (which stood for male fresh water) and Tiamat (which stood for female seawater) (Sandars, 1971, p. 73). From these beings, major and minor gods were created. "As these offspring grow, they begin to order the chaos of the primeval world and assert their unique roles in the cosmos. But as time passes they grow so assertive that they violate the original order established by Apsu and Tiamat" (Dillon, 2010, p. 496). This violation does not sit well with Apsu and Tiamat. Given that they are the originators, they take

---

[4] Although there is ample data about the bases for most of the polarized mentalities discussed in this book, this knowledge is lacking in certain cases. For example, too little is known about elements of ancient Egyptian, Chinese, and Aryan civilizations to directly trace their polarizing roots. That said, one can still make sound inferences about such civilizations based on the backgrounds of many other similarly disposed cultures. These backgrounds converge on one overarching theme: cosmic helplessness as a driving force.

offense at the idea that the younger generation has usurped their powers and created a foreign world order. In reaction to this offense, Apsu plots to kill them. He tells his wife, Tiamat: "Their manners revolt me, day and night without remission we suffer. My will is to destroy them, all of their kind, we shall have peace at last and we will sleep again" (Sandars, p. 74). Despite these declarations however, the lesser gods learn of Apsu's intentions and plot to disrupt him before he can carry them out. One offspring, Ea, finds a way to put Apsu to sleep and drown him.

When Tiamat learns of this assassination, she flies into a rage and vows to avenge it. At first she creates a variety of monsters to seek her vengeance—Kingu being chief among them. Again, however, some of the offspring learn of her strategy and attempt to disrupt it. However, their first attempts fail miserably until eventually they send Ea's son Marduk to defeat Kingu and the other monsters, and he succeeds masterfully. Marduk appears to be a monster of a different order. Here is how he is described:

His limbs were immaculate, the making of a fearful mystery beyond comprehension; with four eyes for limitless sight, and four ears for hearing all; when his lips moved a tongue of fire burst out. Titanic limbs, standing so high he overstepped the tallest god; he was strong and he wore the glory of ten, and their lightnings played round him. (Sandars, p. 76)

In exchange for his termination of Kingu, Marduk is promised to become king of all the gods. While this agreement is fulfilled, Marduk does not cease in his barbarous campaign. In order to fully restore the power of the gods to control and order creation, he sets himself the task of eradicating Tiamat herself. First he "splits her body in half, dividing her power by placing waters above and waters below the earth." Then "he removes her eyes forming the Tigris and Euphrates rivers…and eventually he reorders the "original broken [world] by…building it upon the carcasses of slain divine beings" (Dillon, p. 497). He then puts the new generation of gods in their "rightful" places and presides over a new—and decidedly enduring—world order.

The take-home message of *Enuma Elish* is that for humanity to thrive it must *control* the chaos of existence. While this control can have comparatively constructive dimensions, as in the flexible and yet mildly unstable existence of Apsu and Tiamat, it can also take on malignant, or better yet, polarized forms as embodied in the character of Marduk. Marduk is representative of the leader or culture that feels it must suppress all forms of uncertainty in order to sustain itself. He is the offspring that panics in the face of the groundlessness of being and must inflate himself in order to give the illusion of power and control. On the other hand, he must contract himself in certain ways to avoid the reality (inexorably evident) that he is really not in control. This contraction includes the suppression of others who threaten his position as supreme or who create potentially destabilizing alternatives to his "safe" and familiar regime. In short, *Enuma Elish* is a parable of the repressive aggressor that we have seen repeatedly throughout the history of mystery-denying cultures.

Then there's *The Epic of Gilgamesh.* In this third millennium B.C. treatise, written just after *Enuma Elish,* we revisit the forces of chaos and light, good and evil, human and divine. Very much a precursor to the Western literary canon, *Gilgamesh* is a more elaborate story of the human struggle for greatness, against the bewildering forces of nature and death. Gilgamesh is an ambitious and youthful king. He is also half human and half deity. As the victims of Gilgamesh's exploits grow weary of him, they call on the gods for a companion who can match him in both mentality and strength. This companion is delivered as Enkidu, a "natural man" who is raised by animals. Soon Gilgamesh and Enkidu become close friends and set out on a dramatic journey. This journey takes place in a dark forest amid many strange tribes. The reason for Gilgamesh and Enkidu's journey is simple: they seek cedar wood to bring back to their hometown of Uruk so that they can build great shrines to their gods; however, the outcome of their journey is not so simple.

The tribes and creatures of the forest do all they can to block the protagonists from pursuing their goal. The protagonists, on the other hand, and especially Gilgamesh refuse to be stopped, and call on a god, Shamash, to assist them. Once Shamash secures an agreement from them that they will build a shrine for him, he comes to their aid. This is especially helpful when Gilgamesh and Enkidu encounter the great monster of the forest, Humbaba. While the tribes were mortal, Humbaba seemed invincible, until Shamash intervened. Humbaba in fact was considered "evil," and Gilgamesh and Enkidu took pride in their destruction of that evil. Their mission was succinct: "Because of the evil that is in the land, we will go to the forest to destroy the evil" (Sandars, 1972, p. 33). But what they didn't realize is that because they were interfering with the natural order of things, they were incurring the wrath of other gods that opposed Shamash. One of these gods was Enhil, the storm god. Following what appeared to be a successful conclusion to their journey, Gilgamesh is glorified by his subjects in a dazzling scene of robed and decorated beauty. This image attracted the goddess Ishtar, who wished to take Gilgamesh as her lover. But stirred by the knowledge of her ill-fated past lovers, Gilgamesh spurns her love and incurs her great wrath. To avenge his rejection she sends a monster to him, which he is able to overcome. However, Enkidu was not as fortunate. Still laboring under the power of Humbaba, Enkidu refuses to be humble and is sent to his death in the underworld.

The death of Enkidu triggers a profound reaction within Gilgamesh against the limits of life, in particular his own. Following his command to all the statue makers of the land to create a gold likeness of his friend, Gilgamesh sets out to obtain a complete antidote to death. In a chapter entitled "The Search for Everlasting Life," Gilgamesh's journey is described thusly:

> Bitterly Gilgamesh wept for his friend Enkidu; he wandered over the wilderness as a hunter, he roamed over the plains; in his bitterness he cried, "How can I rest, how can I be at peace? Despair is in my heart. What my brother is now, that shall I be when I am dead. Because I am afraid of death I will go as best I can to find Utnapishtim whom they call the Faraway, for he has entered the assembly of the Gods." And so Gilgamesh traveled over the wilderness, he wandered

over the grasslands, a long journey, in search of [immortality]. (Sandars, p. 97)

But Gilgamesh did not find immortality. What he found was a series of obstacles and warnings about the futility of obtaining immortality, and thusly did his tale unfold. After an extremely arduous journey, Gilgamesh found a plant that was supposed to give everlasting life. But when he stopped at a watering hole on his way back to deliver this plant to his people, and eventually, to consume it himself, a serpent sneaks up on him and snatches it away. With one fell swoop, Gilgamesh's dream and the dreams of so many were abruptly shattered. One of the gods who had at one time been angered but was now tempered by Gilgamesh's ambitions then decreed his fate:

In mother-earth the darkness will show him a light....The heroes, the wise men, like the new moon have their waxing and waning....O Gilgamesh, this was the meaning of your dream. You were given kingship, such was your destiny, everlasting life was not your destiny." (Sandars, p. 118)

The story of Gilgamesh is rich with archetypal imagery. It appears to be the prototype for much of the material in the Old and New Testaments, for Greek and Roman mythology, and for classics of literature, such as Homer's *Odyssey* and Dante's *Inferno*. These points have been well established. However, our focus here is not so much on the literary precedents of Gilgamesh's journey but its implications for the psychology of polarization. As I view it, there are several illuminating themes in this context. The first is that polarization, and the denial of mystery, are extraordinarily seductive. Gilgamesh is a dashing and attractive youth. He is a bold and fearless warrior, and he is a ruler without peer. In short, Gilgamesh represents the "best" that humanity can offer, and he even points beyond the best because he is in part a god. To put it another way, who on earth would *not* want to possess the qualities of a Gilgamesh— strength, attractiveness, intelligence, boldness, and, on top of it, potential (he and we hope) immortality!

But we need to look very closely at these set of traits because, as we shall see, they have formed the bane, as well as the boon, of much that we call humanity. What *Gilgamesh* shows more than tells us is that life is complex. First appearances are often deceiving, and "goodness" can quickly turn into destructiveness the moment it loses touch with that complexity. Gilgamesh's error, the book implies, is not being handsome, brave, and ambitious, but is in making a shrine of those qualities, getting caught up in their luster, and dismissing human vulnerability. The result of his folly, as well as that of Enkidu, is that they leave destruction in their wake and are oblivious to their crimes—until the end, of course, when they suffer the supreme penalty.

The Hebrew Bible

The fixation on singular goals and the obliviousness to criminality as a result are cautionary lessons some years later in the construction of the Hebrew bible. Despite "His" well-deserved reputation for compassion, God (or "the one who cannot be named") also punishes numerous individuals for their attempts to usurp His power, and for their allegiance to lesser deities. On the one hand, this approach led God to outlaw human sacrifice, murder, adultery, idolatry, theft, desecration, and so on. On the other hand, it also ironically appeared to lead God to commit (or sanction the committing of) some of these same desecrations. To wit: His "approval" of stoning, even when lethal, of those who committed infidelities, His oversight of mass slaughter—sometimes of whole nations—and even the slaughtering of factions of His own people. When the Levite Korah led a rebellion against Moses and Aaron over sacred rites, the priestly author relates:

> The glory of Yahweh [God] appeared to the whole congregation. And Yahweh spoke to Moses and to Aaron, saying: Separate yourselves from this congregation, so that I may consume them in a moment. They fell on their faces, and said, "O God, the God of the spirits of all flesh, shall one person sin and you become angry with the whole congregation." (Numbers, 16: 19b–22)

A religious ritual was then shared by the entire congregation that embraced Aaron's version of what was sacred, and due to the intercession of Moses and Aaron, Yahweh forgave the Israelites as a whole for their would-be transgression. However, He still singled out Korah's party for punishment, "implicitly because their offering of incense was offensive and a desecration" (Merker, 2009, p. 155): "And fire came out from Yahweh and consumed the two hundred fifty men offering the incense" (16:35).

Hence, when even the greatest are seen to be vengeful, petty, or capricious, what does this imply for the follower? What kind of models were beginning to be formed about humility, the consideration of individual cases, and the ambiguity of motivations? Although theorists such as Riane Eisler (1987) attribute this narrowness to the onset of Western patriarchy, I surmise that there is more at issue. Yahweh's jealousy, rage, and pursuit of absolute control is not just a male issue; it is an issue that dogs the human race as a whole, particularly when it experiences threat (Huston Smith, personal communication, 4/18/10). The question is: Why do some react more vehemently than others, and how do so many get caught up in that reactivity?

Ancient Greece

We are provided a glimpse into that problem by the rulers and followers of ancient Greece. At the same time that Athenians were developing a proto-democracy and some of the subtlest scholarship known to humanity, they were also mounting some of the most brutal and ambitious war campaigns known to the ancient world. "They are adventurous beyond their power," as the early fifth century B.C.E. historian Thucydides described them, "daring beyond their judgment" (Findlay, 1959, p. 254). In time, these actions became so egregious that a special word was invented to describe them—that word became known as "hubris." Drawing from Homer's depiction of excessive pride, hubris defined the wildly exaggerated belief in one's own greatness. This was the problem for an assortment of Greek politicians, generals, and armies, and it was almost always followed by disaster.

The Greek historian Herodotus explains:

Do you see how God with his lightning smites always the bigger animals, and will not suffer them. How likewise his bolts fall ever on the highest houses and the tallest trees? So plainly does He love to bring down everything that exalts itself. Thus, ofttimes a mighty host is discomfited by a few men, when God in his jealousy sends fear or storm from heaven, and they perish in a way unworthy of them. For God allows no one to have high thoughts but Himself. (cited in Findlay, p. 89)

The question as to how these "high thoughts" arose in ancient Greece, and what made them so menacing is still somewhat open. However, the corresponding Greek notion of "nemesis" can shed light on this problem. Evidently, the calamity of hubris became so menacing in ancient Greek society that a powerful antidote needed to be invoked that drew not only from human but from divine sources of strength. This antidote was called nemesis, which stood for divine retribution or vengeance. The power of nemesis to staunch hubris, however, appears to have been severely hampered by its own hubris-like tendencies. And in the case of wars, blood feuds and other destructive cycles, nemesis itself appears to have become as much of an instigator as the hubris it was conceived to defeat. The almost ceaseless battles between the ancient Greeks and Persians, for example, or between the Athenians and the Spartans somewhat later, are stark examples of this problem and of the fruitlessness, at points, of so-called proportional justice (or nemesis).

The ancient concepts of nemesis and hubris, however, were not confined to Greece, but extended to friend and foe alike. When Xerxes, the young Persian ruler during the late fifth century B.C.E., set out to avenge the death of his father, Darius, at the hands of the Greeks, he proclaimed:

Persians, I shall not be the first to bring in among you this custom—I shall but follow one which has come down to us from our forefathers. Never yet, as our old men assure me, *has our race reposed itself*....Now in all this *God guides us*; and we, obeying his guidance, prosper greatly....But for myself, I will say that, from the day on which I mounted the throne, I have not ceased to consider by what means I may rival those who have preceded me in this post of honor, and *increase the power* of Persia as much as any of them....My intent is to throw a bridge over the Hellenspont and march an army through Europe against Greece, that thereby I may obtain *vengeance* from the Athenians for the wrongs committed by them against the Persians and against my father.... (cited in Findlay, p.85; *emphases mine*)

Thus far, we have witnessed the display of hubris, and by implication polarization, in vengeance (nemesis), in national pride, and in entitlement. But what we have yet to see, and shall witness momentarily, is the concentration of all these elements in one world-conquering culture.

Ancient Rome

"I came, I saw, I conquered." With this simple phrase, Julius Caesar ushered in an entirely new direction not just for ancient Rome but for Western civilization itself. For what Caesar wrought was the singular task of ruling the world. Well before Caesar's leadership, Rome had established a strategy of simply taking over countries, stripping them of ultimate authority, and compelling their allegiance by enabling them to become Roman citizens. This "unite-and-share-the-plunder" policy helped Rome to become a titanic power, with a breathtaking supply of military and civilian resources (Garraty & Gay, 1972, p. 193). But under the leadership of Caesar, what had begun as a regional operation was transformed into a world-encompassing campaign in which Rome's rule stretched from the British Isles to the Near and Middle East by the early part of the first century C.E.

Who was this man who marshaled thousands in the Roman cause of conquest? Who were these people who rallied round him (until he was assassinated, of course)? Suetonius (96/1979), the renowned Roman historian, informs us that though Caesar was brutal with those who opposed him, he was not "naturally" vindictive. Indeed he "would always cheerfully come to terms with his bitterest enemies," when given the chance (p. 44), and he was well known for his affection for his friends. Unlike future Caesars (or rulers), he was not apparently a sadist or a psychopath. Yet he may have had more blood on his hands from expansionist campaigns than virtually any of his successors.

Hence, what were the motives of this enigmatic icon, this otherwise "normal" man? Let us consider a snippet from his biography.

Caesar, it seems, was ambitious from a very early age. His father died when he was 15, and he defied the Dictator Sulla's command to divorce the woman he loved and marry another. As a consequence, Sulla stripped him of his priesthood (acquired as a promising youth), his wife's dowry, and his own inheritance. Further, Sulla drove Caesar underground to avoid the imperial police. And yet despite these hardships—as well illness and isolation—Caesar refused to relent. Eventually, Sulla gave way, saying "There are many Marius's [meaning people like Sulla's archenemy, Marius] in this fellow Caesar" (p. 14).

In time, Caesar's pluck only intensified. As a governor stationed at a statue of Alexander the Great, he was once "overheard to sigh impatiently…that at an age when Alexander had already conquered the whole world, he himself had done nothing in the least epoch-making. Moreover, when on the following night he had a dream of raping his own mother, the soothsayers greatly encouraged him by their interpretation of it: namely, that he was destined to conquer the earth, our Universal Mother" (p. 16).

What then are we to make of these colossal desires and anxieties? What drives a man to lament that he hasn't conquered the entire world by the same age that Alexander the Great had or to embrace a dream of raping his mother as a metaphor for the conquest of Mother Earth? There are no simple answers here, but vengefulness, entitlement, and national pride certainly have to be figured in, as do genetics, gender bias, and cultural belief systems. Each of these acted as blinders, promoters of the fixated mind.

The case of succeeding Roman emperors (or "Caesars" as they came to be called) is hardly more elevating than that of Julius Caesar's, but equally as dramatic. Following Augustus, Julius Caesar's comparatively worthy successor, a whole series of lesser lights ascended the Roman throne. These "lessers" are worthy of scrutiny because, as modern writers have observed, they resemble a personality type that bears perhaps greater familiarity today than it did back when such emperors reigned.

This personality type is marked by three major qualities—shallowness, self-absorption, and resentment. Ortega y Gasset (1932/1960) amplifies:

> ...this impression of a shrinking of vitality, of a falling from position, of decay and loss of pulse shows itself increasingly in the Roman Empire. Had not Horace already sung: "Our fathers, viler than our grandfathers, begot us [children] who are even viler, and we shall bring forth a progeny more degenerate still"? (p. 30)

Such was the case with Gaius (Caligula), Rome's fourth Caesar, and arguably most detestable leader. If Julius Caesar rose to power through hardscrabble struggle, Gaius ascended to his position through treachery and title. Germanicus, Gaius's highly esteemed father, was regaled with affection for his many attractive qualities. As the historian Suetonius explains, he was

> "everywhere described as having been of outstanding physical and moral excellence. He was handsome, courageous, a past-master of Greek and Latin oratory..., conspicuously kind-hearted, and gifted with the powerful desire and capacity for winning respect and inspiring affection. (p.154)

Following Germanicus's death there was a great pall over Rome. The populace as a whole was in mourning. Gaius grew up in this fervor and was raised mainly by the military, who knew much about his father and war but little, it seems, about raising a tempestuous child. Early on, Tiberius, then Caesar of Rome, lamented about Gaius: "I am nursing a viper for the Roman people, and a Phaethon [a Greek god who fell from his chariot and scorched the earth] for the whole world" (p. 158). So "vicious" was Gaius that even as a child he "loved watching tortures and executions; and disguised in wig and robe, abandoned himself nightly to the pleasures of gluttonous and adulterous living" (p. 158). Despite these ominous qualities, after Gaius ascended the throne (following Tiberius's death), he did show some redeeming qualities, such as his funeral oration in honor of Tiberius, his recall of all Roman exiles, and his generosity on holidays. However, as Suetonius inveighs, "So much for the Emperor; the rest of this history must deal with the Monster" (p. 163).

Without belaboring the details of his "monstrous" evolution, suffice it to say that Gaius was as petty, self-important, and resentful as rulers come. One of his first acts, for example, was to treat himself as a god by retrieving "the most famous statues of Greek deities...and having their heads replaced by his own" (p. 164). He also "established a shrine to himself as a god," complete with priests, victims of his power, and a "life-size golden image" of himself (p. 164). He also "frequently had trials by torture held in his presence while he was eating or otherwise enjoying himself" (p. 170), and beheaded, toyed with, and tormented countless underlings, simply by whim. We learn further that Gaius was rather physically unattractive and "because of his baldness and hairiness he announced that it was a capital offence for anyone either to look down on him as he passed or mention goats in any context" (p. 178). As a boy, it seems Gaius was also quite sickly, given to both fits of epilepsy and difficulty walking; and he was notorious for mental instability, which ranged from "overconfidence" to "extreme timorousness" (p. 179).

These qualities all seemed to converge in Gaius's fits of rage when any hint of his vulnerability—his sense of inferiority before creation—came into question. Suetonius underscored Gaius's touchiness on this matter when he elaborated that, "Any good-looking man with a fine head of hair whom Gaius ran across...had the back of his scalp brutally shaved" (p. 17)

The maintenance of superiority, grandness, and dominance, then, would appear to be Gaius's chief project, and he was hardly alone in his proclivities. As noted earlier, subsequent emperors, such as Nero, also shared many of these qualities. While there were certainly redemptive sides to such rulers, their extreme characters seemed to feed off their own failed lives, their own pretense to greatness, even if all about them decay was evident (as was increasingly the case with ancient Rome). What these leaders and their followers came to believe in was their own "reflection" of past glory, not their own hard-earned effort. "Hereditary nobility," Ortega y Gasset acutely observed, "has an indirect character, it is mirrored light...derived from the dead" (p. 64).

That this "mirrored light" resulted in the slaughter of countless innocents, political and religious converts, and foreign vassals is one of the notorious legacies of ancient Rome. That it led to the countless cycles of vengeance, counter-polarizations, and fanaticisms of the evolving contemporary world is another matter entirely—and one which we cannot casually ignore.

The East

Lest we become lulled into the stereotype that most of the above ills are confined to the West, let us consider again. Beginning with ancient Egypt, the Middle and Far East are replete with parallel examples. Take the case of the Pharaoh Ramses II (circa 1310 B.C.E. to 1235 B.C.E.), who ruled Egypt and its surrounding terrain for 67 years. Not only did he father 162 children, but he built a statue of himself that was 66 feet high. Further, he "covered the walls of his enormous temples with vainglorious pictures and inscriptions" and on one of these he wrote: "Look on my works, ye Mighty, and despair!" (Garraty & Gay, 1972, p. 86). Droll to be sure, but I doubt he was joking! And neither were his henchmen joking when they enslaved multitudes and subjugated them to the state, when Hebrews and North Africans were turned into chattel and made to repudiate their folk traditions and rituals, and when all within the Egyptian dominion were required to prostrate themselves before the one and only sun-god, Ra, whose absolute reign was sacrosanct.

Although we lack knowledge about Ramses' background motivations for his grandiosity, we can surmise that they run deep in his personal, and collective, past. As we have seen with similar leaders—e.g., Caesar—such arrogance is not generally arbitrary but predicated on an equivalent and intolerable despair.

Meantime, in another sector of the East, we observe the rise of a very different yet similarly powerful creed. The Hindu religion of India can be traced to Aryan invaders from the north (beginning about 1500 B.C.E.). These Aryan invaders brought with them a formidable military arsenal as well as a set of sacred teachings called "Vedas" that presaged and had a critical influence on the development of many warrior cultures to come.

For example, the Aryans were an "aggressive warrior aristocracy" that "left a common cultural heritage from Greece through Iran into India" (Garraty & Gay, 1972, p. 97). Further, the Aryans displayed an "optimistic" view of life, believing that they could control even the most unruly elements of their environment (p. 98). At the same time, however, these very same conquerors, or "warrior aristocrats" as they came to be called, may have become overly confident about their lot. For example, they evolved a "vast magical technocracy designed to manipulate both the external world and the gods themselves" (p. 98). In a passage from the Brahmanas, one of their early sacred texts, a priest "'compels" the gods to function as one of his agents, demonstrating in no uncertain terms that "the priests are higher than the gods" (p. 98). While we don't know the direct basis for this presumption, we can surmise that it, too, arose from desperation. It is well known that wars, drought, and the lack of tillable land could dispose cultures toward belligerence and pride (see Kaplan, 2012).

Perhaps drawing in part from this presumption, the early Hindus developed their own aristocratic system, complete with sacred teachings, a strict social hierarchy, and sacrifices to teach the populace about the new lineage of political and religious authority (pp. 98–99). According to Smith (1986), by the time of Guatama Buddha (about 550 B.C.E.), Hindu authority, ritual, speculation, and tradition reached an apex of both arrogance and complacency. From Buddha's perspective, for example, Hindu authority "had become a front for the plush privilege of the Brahmin caste. Strict guild regulations had been devised to ensure that religious truth discovered in their culture remain their secret possession" (p. 139). Smith goes on:

> Ritual, instead of providing a warm protecting husk within which the seed of spirit might germinate, had become a confining shell. Endless libations, sacrifices, chants, and musicales were available if one had cash to pay the priest to perform them, but the spirit had largely departed. Speculation was similarly rife—interminable disputes as to whether or not the world had been created, what the upper and nether worlds were like, and what precisely transmigrated after death—but to what end?...Tradition,

instead of conserving and transmitting the wealth of the past, had become a drag on progress....Notions of divine sovereignty and grace had become equally repressive, the latter having been pushed to the false conclusion that nothing needed to be done to effect one's salvation....Finally mystery had degenerated into mystification with magic and divination having all but taken over. Religion had become a technique for cajoling or coercing innumerable cosmic bellhops to do what you wanted them to. (p. 140)

Foundational religious and political traditions of ancient China became no less polarizing. Although ancient China "had been neither more nor less turbulent than other lands" (Smith, p. 224), it certainly had its ongoing hatreds, feuds, and tyrannies. In the earliest of recorded times, beginning around the eighth century B.C.E., China suffered a state of almost "continuous warfare," but it was a "chivalrous" warfare in which the Chariot led men into battle, the code of courtesy was honored, and acts of generosity were highly prized (p. 224). However, by the time of Confucius, arguably China's most influential thinker, war had degenerated into cavalry-led raids, surprise attacks, and merciless treatment of prisoners. Instead of holding prisoners for ransom, for example, as was the practice in earlier times, during Confucius's time, prisoners were being put to death on a mass scale:

> Whole populations unlucky enough to be captured were beheaded, including women, children, and the aged...mass slaughters of 60,000" and more were not unheard of. (p. 224)

What seemed to be happening is that the social structure of China was shifting from one of tradition-bound "herd instinct" to one of reason-inspired "self-interest;" however, the "reason" part did not seem to be leading to a civil society. On the contrary, it seemed to point to a society that no longer knew what to do with itself except to gratify immediate individual needs over those of the social order. There were two basic responses to this breakdown: the cynicism of the Realists, and the optimism of the Mohists (named after the leader of this movement, Mo Tzu). The Realists believed in an "elaborate system" of punishments and rewards to motivate civility. The Mohists on the other hand, 500 years before Christ, believed in love (Smith, p. 230). But the extremes of the two systems, Confucius later observed, promoted distortions of the human experience. For example, the Realists, from Confucius's perspective, dealt largely with external control and as such fostered limited social change. Confucius believed the reason for this was that harsh punishments and high rewards did not give people any substantive rationales for changing their behaviors. As a result, those behaviors might change fleetingly, but the change would not be sustained. He viewed Mohism, conversely, as an appealing ideal but not readily or, in some circumstances, realistically attainable. He viewed justice as a more appropriate response to enmity than love, familial closeness as more realistically attainable then closeness, with all individuals at all times (Smith, p. 235).

The upshot is that polarized living, whether cynical or Pollyannaish could not appreciably shift the destructiveness in ancient China, and many lessons were yet to be learned about the need for a more totalistic view of life.

In early Japan, there were parallel lessons to be learned. From its inception several hundred years B.C.E., the "Domestic Cult of Shinto" (or "the way of the Gods") became the "universal religion in all Japan" (Horner, 1948, pp.11 and 21). This "complex set of beliefs" emphasized one of the most intense forms of ancestral worship known to civilization, and eventually pervaded large numbers of Japanese households. Francis J. Horner, an intimate observer of Japanese culture contended: "One of the essential features of Shinto" was "ritual purity." In this land of cataclysmic geological events, "the avoidance of pollution was a matter of the utmost importance. This idea certainly developed from the primitive conception of death as corruption, and the horror that arose from it" (p. 19).

"With the development of Shinto," Horner continues, "the number of offences which caused pollution increased" (p. 20). There were injunctions against the physically unclean, the impolite, and even the malicious thought—virtually any idea or thing that might offend the departed was prohibited. Based on this quasi-animistic view, Horner elaborated, the departed were believed to possess uncanny powers of oversight. They could "observe all that happens" in the typical Japanese household. Not only could "they hear every whispered word... they [were believed to be able] read thoughts. They represent[ed] the ever-present, all-seeing eye whose scrutiny no member [could] escape" (Horner, pp. 22–23).

Drawing upon this philosophy, the law of filial piety became commonplace in Japanese society. This law or folk tradition—derived in part from ancient Confucianism—embraced "reverence for the dead as well as the sentiment of duty for the living..." (p. 24).

Given these early influences, it is not surprising that historical Japan developed some very polarizing tendencies. The first was known as "emperor worship," which was a highly nationalistic belief in the divine origin of Japan's supreme leader (p. 51). This leader was believed to have derived from the Sun goddess, who conferred her divinity by association to the entire Japanese populace (p. 7). Second, and associated with emperor worship, was the obeisance to the Shogunate or ruling factions of Japan. These leaders became wealthy landowners and oversaw lavish palaces and households. The Shogunate employed samurai as their highly respected, impeccably trained military servants. Remarkably disciplined and literate, the samurai were nevertheless ruthless and kept Japan in check for over 600 years (Keegan, 1993, p. 42). With the samurai at their command, the Shogunate was able to put down virtually all uprisings and invasions; as a result, Japan became a powerful yet isolated nation (Keegan, p. 42). Through the samurai, moreover, the old injunctions against pollution and foreign elements achieved a particular prominence, and other longstanding notions, such as ancestor worship, filial duty, and indifference to physical hardship were similarly reinforced. With the advent of Buddhism in the sixth century C.E., the Shogunate found a new path to merge with and reinforce their ancient folkways. For although Buddhism, and in particular the Japanese version of Zen, opened minds and discouraged doctrines, it was also used to bolster ancestor worship and improve military discipline (Keegan, p. 45).

Eventually, the Shogunate merged into one overarching government that reigned for about 200 years. During this time (from the late 1600s to the late 1800s), it fought off two major foreign invasions—the incursion of Christianity via Portuguese missionaries and the arrival of Commodore Perry in Tokyo Bay in 1854—dangers which the Shogunate eradicated with dispatch. But, as will be elaborated later, the effect of the invasions, in concert with longstanding cultural traditions, only served to radicalize. The tendencies to close ranks around its own leadership, to believe in the purity and divinity of that leadership, and to avenge the threats to that leadership attained an unprecedented status—culminated in a catastrophe of epic proportions on the streets of Nanking and later Hiroshima and Nagasaki. This, then, was the price to be paid for a culture that profoundly and innocently longed to be embraced by its ancestry, that accorded divinity to its ancestry, and that shattered in disillusionment when it became apparent that its ancestry could not always keep it safe. According to noted psychiatrist Takeo Doi, the Japanese both flourished and yet floundered by their need for what he called "amae" or "passive love" (21). The love of the Sun goddess, or the ruler, or the family could all be relied on except when the limits of these authorities became increasingly evident through, for example, modernization and contact with the outside world, with increasingly problematic results. Doi (1971) put it this way:

> I defined amae as being in the first place the craving of the newborn child for close contact with its mother, and in the broader sense, the desire to deny the fact of separation that is an inevitable part of human existence, and to obliterate the pain that this separation involves. (p. 167)

Yet to obliterate the pain of separation is also to obliterate the potential growth of—as well as need for—separation, which in the end is a recipe for totalitarianism. Japan then, like all of the cultures previously discussed, remains an object lesson; for through its fears of geological upheaval, uncertainty, and death, it holds another mirror up to us regarding the terror and resultant denial of mystery-laden existence.

Chapter 2

Successors to Polarization:
More Recent Denials of Mystery
Through History

As we have seen, the ancient power centers of the world, have inspired some of the most debilitated life philosophies known to humanity—right alongside their splendor. These life philosophies, moreover, have sown the seeds for many succeeding generations of mystery-denying cultures, a sampling of which we will consider presently.

The Christian Empire
The synod (assembly of church delegates) at Constantinople in approximately 325 C.E., was the culmination of one of the greatest conquests in religious history. At that fateful meeting, the most powerful bishops in Western Civilization—which at that time was a *Roman* civilization—delineated the Christian faith. This delineation was made despite the establishment of a wide array of Christian creeds both within and outside the empire at the time. These creeds each had their own literature, conceptions of Christ, and congregational structure (Pagels, 1979). The declaration was also made by a handful of men who served essentially at the pleasure of the newly Christianized ruler of the Roman empire, Constantine.

By the same token, there was nothing really surprising about this "sudden" declaration of Christian orthodoxy; the seeds of its development can be traced to the largely urban, predominantly aristocratic Roman superstructure that had long been skillful at administering to and dominating a pastoral frontier. Furthermore, although many of the various Christian creeds of the time used a range of means to promote their own time-honored perspectives, the orthodox (or Roman Catholic) contingent appeared to have perfected these means, above and beyond the rest. First, they had some of the most articulate spokespeople, such as Paul of Tarsus, to broadcast their message; second, they mobilized their considerable power to persuade churches of other denominations to ignore or remove those who taught contrasting points of view; third, they forged documents in the name of Jesus's apostles to support their point of view; fourth, they sometimes modified "heretical" texts to make them sound more orthodox; and fifth, they began selecting books that they declared to be accurate reflections of the gospels and excluded other books as heretical forgeries (Bauer, 1971; Ehrman, 2002).

One of the chief spokespeople for the Christian orthodoxy was a Roman bishop (of Lyon) named Irenaeus. In circa 180 C.E., Irenaeus pronounced confidently that the Catholic Church

> believes these [unified] points of doctrine just as if she had one soul, and one and the same heart, and she proclaims them and teaches them in perfect harmony....For although the languages of the world are different, still the meaning of the tradition is one and the same. (Pagels, p. 28)

He goes on to consider the question of who or what body should settle disputes of doctrinal discord, and decides definitively that it should be an "ancient" and "universally known" church, namely, Rome:

> Suppose a dispute concerning some important question arises among us; should we not have recourse to the most ancient churches, with which the apostles held continual intercourse, and learn from them what is clear and certain with regard to the present question? (p. 29)

He ends the debate by indicating that tradition, derived from the apostles,

> of the very great, the very ancient, and the universally known church organized and founded at Rome by the two most glorious apostles, Peter and Paul...which came down to our time by means of the succession of bishops...[is the church] that every church should agree with...on account of its preeminent authority. (p.29)

Yet it was clear that not all Christian creeds agreed with Iranaeus's stance, and at least some among them called Gnostics (who believed in a nonhierarchical view of God) accused the orthodox of denying the "mystery" of God. In a passage from one of their texts, the risen Christ informs Peter that those who call "themselves bishop, and also deacon, as if they had received their authority from God" are in actuality "waterless canals. Although they 'do not understand mystery,' they 'boast that the mystery of truth belongs to them'" (Pagels, p. 29).

Another of the archetypal successors to mystery denial was the Crusades. In 1099 A.D., Pope Urban II looked about him and saw widespread strife: Christians fighting Christians, Christians fighting Muslims, and emperors such as Henry the IV of Germany being "cast out of the Church because he had challenged Papal authority" (Phillips, 2009, p. 4).

Yet for Pope Urban the "answer" to this chaotic scenario was not a simple one. Direct force through Church dogma did not seem very effective with these various splinter groups, and there was a growing concern about a crisis in Christian faith. Hence, like few before him, Urban developed a highly sophisticated public relations campaign to rally the Christian masses and restore order and faith. He achieved this through three principal means: the institution of a pilgrimage to the Holy Land of Jerusalem, the declaration of a holy war against those (principally Moslem) who opposed the Christian conquest of the Holy Land, and the offer of salvation to all pilgrims who were willing to brave the mortal dangers of embarking on such a pilgrimage (p. 4). Here is what he said to his constituents by means of a papal edict:

A grave report has come from the lands around Jerusalem...that a race absolutely alien to God...has invaded the land of the Christians....They have either razed the churches of God to the ground or enslaved them to their own rites....They cut open the navels of those whom they choose to torment...drag them around and flog them before killing them as they lie on the ground with all their entrails out....What can I say of the appalling violation of women? On whom does the task lie of avenging this, if not on

you?...Take the road to the Holy Sepulchre, rescue that land
and rule over it yourselves, for that land, as scripture says,
floweth with milk and honey." (Phillips, p. 3)

While it is enough that this language is "hugely exaggerated,"
according to a leading historian of the era, Jonathon Phillips (p. 3),
the Pope went beyond simply magnifying the situation in
Jerusalem and assured all those who would obey his call that the
"unfading glory of the kingdom of heaven" awaited them (p. 3).

Needless to say, this papal edict mobilized thousands of
willing participants, not the least of whom were venturesome
knights, and in relatively short order claimed the lives of
multitudes,—and eventually, up to the time of the Spanish
Inquisition in the late 1400s, untold more. While there were no
simple "good guys" and "bad guys" in this archetypal world
conflict, the bitterness of its legacy was felt early on in the
Islamic world. This bitterness was recorded by a series of
Islamic writers, who ironically sounded very much like the
Christian leaders in their vitriol and religious zeal. To wit:

> The unbelief of the infidels has declared it lawful to
>   inflict harm on Islam, causing prolonged lamentation
>   for the faith.
> What is right is null and void and what is forbidden is [now]
>   made licit.
> The sword is cutting and blood is spilt.
> How many Muslim men have become booty?
> And how many Muslim women's inviolability has been
>   plundered?
> How many a mosque have they made into a church!
> The cross has been set up in the mihrab [prayer niche].
> The blood of the pig is suitable for it.
> Korans have been burned under the guise of incense.
> Do you not owe an obligation to God and Islam,
> Defending thereby young men and old?
> Respond to God: woe on you! Respond! (p. 30)

This tit-for-tat, good-for-bad mentality and proselytizing is
just one of the numerous horrific legacies emanating from the
time of the Crusades. We feel its chill even now in the wake of

U.S. president George Bush's proclamation that the "war on terror" ignited by the Al Qaeda attack on the World Trade center in 2001 was to become a "crusade" (Phillips, p. xxi).

The Inquisition and the Rise of Imperial Spain

Spain and Portugal in the mid-to-late fifteenth century became the power centers of the Western world. Just prior to this development, a large part of Spain was occupied by a comparatively tolerant and culturally diversified regime. This regime was headed by the Castilian King Alfonso X (1252–84), who broke off from papal influence and initiated a series of political and scientific reforms that transformed the medieval world. One of his main accomplishments was to bridge Christian, Jewish, and Islamic heritages by publishing the Koran and Talmud in Latin. He also supported significant translations of Arabic astronomy that would "guide the study of astronomy for the next 200 years" (Reston, 2005, p. 5).

Despite these remarkable reforms, which in some ways echoed the transient tolerance of preceding Muslim conquerors, the major thrust of world power moved toward those who allied with papal authority.   King Ferdinand and Queen Isabella (1479–1504) of Spain were the examples par excellence of this overriding influence.   Both extraordinarily devout, Ferdinand and Isabella initiated one of the bloodiest and most egregious campaigns in all of Christendom—the expulsion of all Jews, including Marranos (converted Jews accused of "backsliding"), from Spanish territory on penalty of death.   Hints of this extremism manifested in Isabella's earlier life with her identification with the watchword of St. John the Evangelist: "Make me passionately virtuous in your image and zealous for the faith" (Reston, p. 54).

Ferdinand and Isabella's official decree, based on a seriously trumped-up charge by their handpicked Grand Inquisitor of the Holy Roman Empire, Tomas de Torquemada (who ironically had Jewish blood in his lineage), read as follows:

> The Jews of Spain are seducing faithful Christians to their own damnable beliefs and opinions, instructing them on the ceremonies and observances of Jewish law, holding meetings

where they read to them and teach them what to believe....
giving them to understand that there is no true law except the
Law of Moses. (Reston, p. 259)

"To this end," the monarchs declared

we issue our Edict, by virtue of which we command all Jews,
of both sexes and all ages, who live...in our kingdoms....be
gone from all our kingdoms and our lands....And not
presume to return...under pain of death.... (p. 259)

As suggested previously, Ferdinand and Isabella were not
the only zealous leaders of a Christianized Spain. Pope Innocent
VIII and the notorious Tomas Torqeumada were equally, and in
some cases surpassingly, extreme. The founder of the Spanish
Inquisition, as it has come to be known, Torqeumada spared no
resources to develop the most formidable Christian police force
known to history. The Inquisition not only enforced the
expulsion of Jews and Muslims from all Spanish territories, but
traveled extensively to root out heresy and extract confessions
wherever heresy was reported. The means at the Inquisitor's
disposal were not only some of the severest forms of torture
known at the time but highly inflamed rhetoric, the
dissemination of rumor, and the stoking of communal fears, as
illustrated above, by Torquemada.

That same fateful year of 1492 saw the launching of
Columbus's ships for the New World, the express purpose of
which, in Columbus's own words, was to support the
"Catholic Princes" as "propagators" of the "Holy Christian
faith" and "enemies of the sect of Mohamet and...all
Idolatries and heresies." (Reston, p. 254)

That Columbus made good on his promise to Ferdinand and
Isabella to "purify the world of heresy and idolatry" (Reston, p.
254) was attested to by a brash landing on the Bahama Islands.
In describing the Arawaks, the indigenous people of these
Islands whom he called "Indians," Columbus wrote: "They
brought us parrots and balls of cotton and spears and many other
things....They willingly traded everything they owned....They
have no iron. Their spears are made of cane....They would make

fine servants....With fifty men we could subjugate them all and make them do whatever we want" (Zinn, 2003, p. 1).

In Columbus's report to Madrid upon his return, he wrote: The Indians "are so naïve and so free with their possessions that no one who has not witnessed them would believe it" (p. 3). In conclusion, he asserted to his royal patrons that, if provided with further support, he would bring back "as much gold as they need...and as many slaves as they ask" (p.4). This euphoric description of his exploits was matched by his certainty about divine guidance. "Thus the eternal God, our Lord, gives victory to those who follow His way over apparent impossibilities" (p. 4).

Recap on the Christian Empire

What, then, are we to make of the rise of Christian imperialism in the early to late medieval world? It seems to me that several lessons are evident here, and each is a case study in the repressed oppressiveness or fearful pomposity to which we alluded earlier. Consider, for example, that the early Christian Church arose out of the humiliation it suffered at the hands of the ancient Roman Empire. While the early Church floundered in those trying periods, the synod of Constantinople was its "release valve," at which time it closed ranks, monopolized doctrine, and consolidated imperial power. The call for a crusade by Pope Urban in 1099 was forged under similar circumstances of infighting, deflated congregants, and flagging Christian power. However, with the advent of Urban's call for a crusade, the entire situation began to reverse. Christian congregants pulled together, the aristocracy rallied around a cause, and the empire reinvigorated its dominions. Certainty was restored, and difference, ambiguity, and inquiry vanquished with dispatch.

The rise of imperial Spain coincided with a similarly weakened religious and political environment. Muslim caliphs had controlled vast portions of formerly Christian lands, and the new Spanish leadership was ripe for establishing its power. King Ferdinand, for example, was eager to assert himself as a young monarch who by dint of dynastic succession became secondary in power to his wife and queen, Isabella; and Isabella—who had long labored under the dictates of her recently deceased half-brother, and erstwhile king, Enrique IV—

was anxious to assert her power as a female leader. These struggles, along with the demands imposed upon them by the Catholic Church, appeared to bolster the monarchs' intolerance, prejudice, and striving for world domination.

Martin Luther and the Protestant Reformation

As the world of Christendom expanded but still reeled from its expulsions, crusades, and depletion of resources, the Catholic Church became increasingly involved in international finance. To fund its myriad operations and maintain its position as a power broker, the Church developed schemes to enrich its overseers. One of these schemes was the selling of indulgences. Indulgences were the full or partial remission of punishments due for sins that had already been forgiven. Prior to indulgences, the Church authorities required a range of punishments, sometimes quite severe, for a correlative range of (moderate to mortal) sins.

Although the indulgences were ostensibly granted for an assortment of "good works" and prayers, a number among the clergy required payment for them, which engendered increasing societal resentment. Increasing numbers of Christians became disillusioned with the Church hierarchy. The feeling seemed to be that although the papacy and its representatives appeared to be faithful messengers of Christ, they also became progressively dictatorial and manipulated themselves into positions of great wealth and power.

As the transparency of this clerical corruption surfaced, a smattering of protests arose, the most prominent of which was led by a voluble and zealous Church scholar named Martin Luther (1483–1546). So much has been written about Luther's life and influence, but what is most important for our purposes here is how that life and influence impacted the polarized mind—both his own and the populace with which he resonated.

Luther's main claim to fame were his brilliantly articulated, intricately argued theses which condemned the centralized authority of the Church, and by implication the papacy itself. Without centralized Church authority, Luther argued, no human intermediary could foul the teachings of Christ; and to the extent that those teachings became purified, then the relations among people would also purportedly become purified. Hence, the end of the selling of indulgences, the end of papal self-aggrandizement, the end of Church profiteering, and so on. Luther earnestly believed that if people followed their own (Christian) conscience and not any human representative of that conscience then they would find their way to a wholesome and merciful life. His courage in fostering those beliefs—despite withering threats to his life—is without peer.

The problem, however, is that during key periods Luther's own life was anything but wholesome and merciful—and his interpretations of scripture too often followed suit. As Erik Erikson (1958) elaborated, along with his genius and ability to inspire, Luther exhibited "suspiciousness, obsessive scrupulosity, moral sadism," and "an extraordinary ability to hate..." (pp. 61 and 65).

Additionally, Luther somehow found justification in biblical scripture to support German princes in their slaughter of some 100,000 peasants during the Peasant War of 1525. At the height of his influence, he also wrote a 65,000 word anti-Semitic screed called "On the Jews and Their Lies" that later "inspired" Nazi propagandists during the Nuremburg rallies. This tract, which too often reads like a forerunner to Hitler's *Mein Kampf*, contains passages calling Jews a "base, whoring people" whose "boast of lineage, circumcision, and law must be accounted as filth" and contends that they are "full of the devil's feces...which they wallow in like swine." The volume calls Jewish synagogues "incorrigible whores" and pleads for Jewish schools to be set on fire, Jewish prayer books to be destroyed, Jewish clergy to be prohibited from preaching, and Jewish homes to be leveled. Even murder is not beyond his invective when he writes that "we are at fault in not slaying [the Jews]." Luther's apparent justification for this inflammatory attack? His disillusionment that Jews did not see the light of his prophesies and convert to Protestantism (See http://en.wikipedia.org/wiki/ Martin_Luther_and_antisemitism for an elaboration on these points.)

That said, Luther was a complex character, whose life reflected profoundly the life of the culture that surrounded him. For example, a notable portion of Luther's behavior can be traced to his tumultuous relationship with his father, who apparently beat him senseless on occasions and held him to an excessively high standard of anti-proletarian elitism (Erikson, 1958). Like many fathers of his generation, but more pronounced, Luther's father imposed an iron will on his son, pressing him to reject his peasant roots and to become the elite, managerial leader that the father himself was not able to become. But this was not at all what Luther envisioned for himself, and the resultant clash of wills instilled an intense resentment in Luther—not only toward his father but toward any authority that he perceived to arbitrarily impose its will.

In a parallel development, Luther's world was also restless over and resentful of the imposition of authority. The "father" Church, which had begun from humble stock, had also become prideful and abusive of its power. This abuse led its congregants astray and, like Luther in the face of his father, relegated them to a bewildering impotency about what to believe and to whom to turn. However, with the Protestant Reformation, both Luther and the populace found their cause, averted their helplessness, and rallied their determination. At the same time, Luther and a number of his followers also rallied their capacity for vengeance, and for "straightening out" all that had been "corruptible." Alongside their reforms, in other words, a number of them also became zealots, *warriors* for certainty and faith. Former victims among them became perpetrators as they in turn not only exacted their revenge on those who opposed or disagreed with them (e.g., the pope, clergy, peasants, and Jews) but also *became* the oppressors whom they had previously spurned.

The story of Luther and elements of the Reformation, then, extends the story of existential helplessness. It furthers the saga of terror in the face of the groundlessness of existence and imperiousness as a compensation for that terror. Neither Luther nor a faction of his followers could wholly wrest themselves from its grip, and neither Luther nor a legacy he fostered could pause at key points and reassess.

The British Empire: Colonial Colossus
Arising from the ashes of Roman, Viking, and Norman conquests, the English monarchs of the Renaissance bristled with ambition. However, in the wake of the Spanish domination of

military, financial, and territorial sectors of the world, England chafed under a new rivalry. King Ferdinand and Queen Isabella had stretched the Spanish and Holy Roman Empire across the globe from West Africa to the Americas and asserted it as a sea power of unparalleled magnitude. But more important, from the standpoint of England and its allies, Spain dominated world commerce, and increasingly the nation that dominated markets dominated the world (Ferguson, 2003). Although England made some early attempts to thwart this Spanish encroachment, these attempts were modest and had little lasting effect. For example, England engaged Spain in some sea battles but was generally outgunned. England also commissioned a few sailing expeditions to the Americas but with limited results.

The tide began to turn, however, in the late 1500s when Elizabeth I sanctioned piracy as a major wartime weapon. Gradually, but with relentless determination, English pirates attacked and outmaneuvered Spanish fleets. Along with a rapidly evolving English naval presence, these pirates helped to induce major Spanish casualties and take over strategic holdings, particularly in the Americas. However, their biggest aims were not just lands or populations but the acquisition of gold. As England developed increasingly sophisticated naval capacities (such as its remarkable defeat of the Spanish Armada), it also cultivated an equally refined capacity for spending and investing in capital markets. This financial power, borrowed from the Dutch, provided England with resources that far exceeded those of the Spanish, and eventually elevated them to the status of a world power. Whereas the rest of the world had to rely on direct payments for the exchange of goods, England learned the art of borrowing on credit, and borrowing on credit, as we know so well today, significantly extends resources. As early as the 1720s, the acute English social observer Daniel Defoe wrote:

> Credit makes war, and makes peace; raises armies, fits our navies, fights battles, besieges towns; and in a word, it is more justly called the sinews of war than money itself...Credit makes the soldier fight without pay, the armies march without provisions...it is an impregnable fortification...it makes paper pass for money...and fills the

Exchequer and the banks with as many millions as it pleases, upon demand. (cited in Ferguson, p. 19)

The cultivation of cheap credit, then, along with a rapidly improving navy and industrial sector, enabled England to project its power to unprecedented regions of the globe. The merger with the Dutch, the conquest of Spain, and the growing influence of British enterprises in the Americas, the West African slave trade, and India all yielded remarkable military and financial gains.

However, by the early 1700s, a new menace arose—France. Although Britain had become the "dominant" naval power in Europe (apart from the Dutch), and could rightly be called an empire (Ferguson, p. 25), France, too, had been steadily acquiring stature. Like England, France had major interests in Canada, in parts of the Americas, and India. As Ferguson (2003) put it, "The struggle with France—which was to rage in every corner of the globe like a worldwide version of the Hundred Years War— would decide who would *govern* the world" (p. 25). By the mid 1700s, the struggle with France reached a peak, and the rhetoric of the time sounds eerily familiar today. Here's how one observer put it in a 1756 article in Britain's *Critical Review:*

Every Briton ought to be acquainted with the ambitious views of France, her eternal thirst after universal dominion, and her continual encroachments on the properties of her neighbors...[O]ur trade, our liberties, our country, nay all the rest of Europe, [are] in a continual danger of falling prey to the common Enemy, the universal Cormorant, that would, if possible, swallow up the whole globe itself. (Ferguson, pp. 25–26)

By 1757, the hostilities between Britain and France ignited, and The Seven Years War, which has been compared to an eighteenth century world war, commenced. Although the fallout of that war is well known—mass casualties, depletion of the treasury, and ultimate British domination (Ferguson, p. 30)— what is less well known is the scale of the outcome and its harrowing result: the conquest of India. India gave Britain "a huge market" and "an inexhaustible reservoir of military manpower" (p. 30). It also provided one of the clearest examples of Britain's polarized mind. The presumption of British political leadership of the time could hardly be overstated. In their overriding view, India was a treasure trove, ripe for the picking. Like Columbus in his arrogance toward Native Americans, British leaders presumed to have bragging rights with Indians, for how else to view their "merciful" reforms? In 1764, Robert Clive, one of the lead commanders of the commercial juggernaut, the East India Company, wrote the following to his board of directors:

> I can assert with some degree of confidence that this rich and flourishing kingdom may be totally subdued by so small a force as two thousand Europeans... [The Indians are] indolent, luxurious, ignorant and cowardly beyond all conception... [They] attempt everything by treachery rather than force... What is it, then, can enable us to secure our present acquisitions or improve upon them but such a force as leaves nothing to the power of treachery and ingratitude? (Ferguson, p. 31)

To be sure, the intervention in India was not entirely dictatorial. It did have benevolent aspects (at least to many Western observers), such as the efforts to curtail "satti," or the ritual burning of widows on funeral pyres, or the occasional cases of female infanticide. However, the problem was not the understandable objections to these extreme and sometimes magnified forms of behavior, but the propagandistic purposes and the ends they often served. These ends comprised two basic dimensions—"the evangelical desire to convert India to Christianity and the Liberal desire to convert [India] to capitalism," so that both morality and wealth echoed British designs.

Consider, for example, the preamble to petitions by Evangelicals all throughout Britain, urging "a speedy and universal promulgation' of Christianity 'throughout the regions of the East" (Ferguson, p. 113), and this starkly demonizing elaboration:

The inhabitants of the populous regions of India which form
an important portion of the British Empire, being involved in
the most deplorable state of moral darkness and under the
influence of the most abominable and degrading superstions,
have a pre-eminent claim on the compassionate feelings and
benevolent services of British Christians. (Ferguson, p. 113)

Lest it appear that such patronizing debasements emanated
only from pamphlets of the pious, consider equally the
pronouncements of one of the most liberal representatives of
academia—John Stuart Mill. He wrote that it was in the "best
interests" of Britain's African and Asian colonies that they
benefit from Britain's "better government" and "improvement of
the public intelligence." Sounding more like a guru of marketing
than a philosopher, he elaborated that this superior society will
reverse "the decay of usages and superstitions which interfere
with the effective implementation of industry; and the growth of
mental activity, making people alive to new objects of desire"
(p.115).

By early 1918, Britain had become one of the most powerful
empires in world history. Its predominance extended from
Europe to large parts of Africa to India and the Americas. While
there were many salutary elements of Britain's imperial reign, its
lessons for mystery denial should not be overlooked. Through
its moralizing evangelical zeal, coupled with narrow mercantile
interests, much of the world has been shaped, and its legacy
remains fresh.

The French Revolution and Napoleon
Sometimes the polarized mind associates with revolutions that
purport to oppose polarized minds, or that begin with corrective
intentions but end with devastating—and equally polarizing—
results. Such was largely the case with the French Revolution
and the period abruptly following, known as "The Terror."

Spurred by a withering legacy of aristocratic rule, the French
Revolution (1789) was an outpouring of public and private rage.
Comprised largely of intellectual elites along with impoverished
townsfolk, the revolution was one of most massive—and
influential—demonstrations of social transformation in the

modern era. The revolution was also inspired by Enlightenment philosophy, which stressed the power of intellect and rationality, egalitarian principles, representative government, and individual freedom. It was designed precisely to oppose the debasing poverty of the time, the disenfranchisement of the working people of the country and the indulgences of the nobility (Davies, 2009). It was also designed to counter the attitude of legislators of the "old regime," who characterized class division and hierarchy as both "natural" and divine (p. 13), and who declared through one of their representatives: "It is necessary that there be order in all things, for their well being and for their direction" (p. 13). This representative, a lawyer named Loyseau, went on to state that

> Because we cannot live together in equality of condition, it is necessary that some command and others obey....Thus by means of these multiple divisions and subdivisions...there is a good harmony and consonance, and a correspondence and interconnectedness from the highest to the lowest, in such a way that through order a numberless variety is led to unity." (cited in Davies, p. 13)

But this attitude, typical of the so-called first and second estates of France that represented the king, clergy, and nobility, was rapidly losing credibility, and a new power structure arose. Led by philosophers like Rousseau and Voltaire, and political intellectuals like Robespierre, the Enlightenment-inspired revolt cut deeply into the fabric of French society until it spilled over on July 14, 1789 with the storming of the Bastille, a royal arsenal in the center of Paris.

Although profoundly emancipating pronouncements were made about the restructuring of feudal–royal society—including the landmark "Declaration of the Rights of Man," which paralleled the U.S. "Bill of Rights"—the more prominent feature of the period was rage. Rage and vengeance appeared to have trumped the intellectualized plans of the revolution's founders and dominated the actions of the day. Even the chief legislative body of the revolution, the Committee for Public Safety, could not avert the polarized contagion. On September 17, 1793, this

body decreed the Law of Suspects, which gathered within it
every bit of the narrowness, paranoia, and absolutism that had
issued from the former regimes they had so vehemently opposed.
Included in this law was the following:

> 2. Immediately after the publication of the present decree, all
> suspected persons within the territory of the Republic and
> still at liberty shall be placed under custody.
> 3. The following are deemed suspected persons: 1st, those
> who, by their conduct, accusations, talk, or writings have
> shown themselves partisans of tyranny or federalism and
> enemies of liberty; 2nd, those who are unable to
> justify...their means of existence and the performance of
> their civic duties; 3rd, those to whom certificates of
> patriotism have been refused. (Davies, p. 71)

What is becoming clear is that, increasingly, the new
inheritors of state are losing their centeredness and becoming
demonic. By demonic I mean, following Tillich (1952), that
they elevated a part of themselves to the utter neglect and
dismissal of other, potentially competing parts. Their definition
of "suspected persons" became so broad as to include virtually
anyone who questioned the revolution. This demonization
seized greater and greater elements of French society and
unleashed a fury of demonic acts. Approximately 40,000 people
became victims of The Terror (Davies, 2009, p. 69), and
countless others left the republic as crowds and lynch mobs
stormed through residences and holdings of the wealthy. King
Louis the XVI was executed in 1793, and soon after his wife,
Queen Marie Antoinette, suffered the same fate. Because of its
steamrolling nature, the "leveling" policies of the revolutionary
government led to devastating consequences in politics, religion,
and the economy. In a move reminiscent of modern day
communist tactics, Robespierre even attempted to enforce a new
religious consciousness on the people. In 1794, Robespierre set
forth the idea of a Supreme Being to "replace" the Christian
deity (Davies, p. 73). A decree soon followed:

> The French people recognizes [sic] the existence of the
> Supreme being and the immortality of the soul....It

recognizes that the proper worship of the Supreme Being consists in fulfilling...duties....It places at the forefront of these duties: to abominate bad faith and tyranny [a euphemism for the royalist ideology], to punish tyrants and traitors, to succor the needy, to respect the weak, to defend the oppressed.... (p. 73)

Moreover this new religion obligated people to a whole series of state-sponsored festivals, which in the words of the authors of the decree, will "take their names from the glorious events of our Revolution, from the virtues dearest to man and most useful to him....Every year the French Republic will celebrate the festivals...." (p. 73).

That trumped-up rhetoric and policy became rampant by this stage of the revolution is indubitable. But the larger and more important question for our analysis is why? What seized the consciousness of so many that they became almost fascist in their anti-fascist stance? Again, I believe we need to look at historical convergences to address this question. By the time of the revolution, the people of France had reached a peak of inconsolability. Poverty was rampant, feudalism and tyranny abounded, and class distinctions were abominable, as witnesses of the unabashed opulence of the Palace at Versailles even today can grasp. At the same time, intellectual leaders who reflected this mass mentality shared at some profound level the same experience of indignation. This was acutely true in the case of Robespierre, who struggled for much of his earlier life as a victim and fierce opponent of royalist domination. The convergence of populist outrage and intellectual disillusionment made for a highly potent brew, and the two elements exploded on an epic and agonizing scale.

The question of ontological insecurity (or insignificance before creation) cannot be discounted as a notable factor in the over-compensatory excesses of the French revolutionaries. Robespierre, for example, lost his mother at the age of six and his father essentially deserted the family. Robespierre was thenceforth brought up in a series of foster homes and assumed many of the duties of caretaker for his two remaining siblings. His sister was quoted as saying that "by virtue of the fact that he was the oldest [child]," Robespierre became "sober, serious and hardworking" (cited in Matrat, 1901, p. 14). It is not a far stretch to assume as one scholar did (see McLetchie, 1984) that what Robespierre brought to his family he also imposed upon the French state, and that his "seriousness" in time became a kind of intractable self-righteousness as a bulwark against the anxieties of helplessness, death, and the unknown.

Napoleon, who claimed the status of emperor in 1804 and reversed some of the key provisions of the revolution, also exhibited traits of compensatory grandiosity. His short stature, coupled with a modest family lineage in comparison to the pedigrees of his aristocratic schoolmates, greatly addled him (Garraty & Gay, 1972). Like Robespierre, he appeared to compensate for these insecurities by developing a powerful and dominating character, and by approaching his convictions as absolute. Garraty and Gay elaborate:

> Napoleon's small size and Corsican accent subjected him to taunts from boys at Brienne [a royal school for sons of nobles], and his unimpressive lineage brought him up against the snobbish contempt of the cadets in Paris. But he was ambitious, hard working and brilliantly successful....(p. 776)

Again, as with Robespierre at the start of the revolution, Napoleon's confidence and smug self-righteousness was as timely as could be. Just as Napoleon ascended as a great military hero, the revolutionary leadership was in disarray. The beloved founders of the revolution such as Danton, and even Robespierre himself, had been executed. In addition, the governing factions such as the Thermadors and Directors, Jacobins, and Girondins continually competed with one another for ultimate control, while the populace reeled from fragmentation and unrest. Napoleon, strong-arm extraordinaire, fresh from his victory in Italy, seized the reins of power in increments. If the pre-Napoleonic, revolutionary era was distinguished by its unruliness, the Napoleonic era was marked by lock-step regimentation.

In his own words, Napoleon observed:

Among so many conflicting ideas and so many different perspectives, the honest man is confused and distressed and the skeptic becomes wicked... Since one must take sides, one might as well choose the side that is victorious, the side which devastates, loots, and burns. Considering the alternative, it is better to eat than to be eaten. [Letter to his brother, as quoted in *The Age of Napoleon* (2002) by J. Christopher Herold, p. 8]

In an address to members of the Catholic clergy, he pronounced:

"I am a monarch of God's creation, and you reptiles of the earth dare not oppose me. I render an account of my government to none save God and Jesus Christ." [Addressing members of the Catholic clergy assembled during "Bonaparte's Conference with the Catholic and Protestant clergy at Breda," May 1, 1810 (originally reported in the Gazette of Dorpt), as quoted in *The life of Napoleon Bonaparte, emperor of the French: with a preliminary view of the French revolution*, Sir Walter Scott, Philadelphia: Leary & Getz, 1857, p. 91]

Finally, in a note about conflict resolution, he quipped: "When you have an enemy in your power, deprive him of the means of ever injuring you" (http://simple.wikiquote.org/wiki/Napoleon_Bonaparte).

That said, Napoleon, like each of the polarized figures heretofore discussed, was hardly one-dimensional. He certainly could be viewed as a "world historical" figure who instigated constructive reforms stemming from the French Revolution, including "equality of men before the law, the rights of citizens, the abolition of manorial privileges" and a new "centralized" form of government that prefigured modern Western society (Garraty & Gay, p. 782).

Still, one is hard-pressed to neglect Napoleon's glaring despotism, his iron-fisted rule, and his military tyranny. Napoleon's arrogance, coupled with French society's disarray, converged to form one of the most mystery-blind mentalities known to pre-nineteenth century Europe.

The Soviet Empire

Following Napoleon's disastrous campaign and ultimate defeat at Waterloo, two major powers rushed in to fill the vacuum: Britain to the West, and, more gradually, Russia to the East. (The United States was also on the rise but did not make its strongest claims to empire until post World War II).

Along with its many treasured heritages, such as literature and music, Russia has long fostered authoritarian rule. From Ivan the Terrible to Peter the Great to Tsar Nicholas II to Lenin and Stalin, "centralized administrative order [was] vital to the country's well-being" (Service, 2009, p. xxvi). Russia's imperialist tendencies were also well documented. On a trip to Russia in 1884, the French author, Vicomte de Vogue called Russia the "America of the East" and wrote: "In our country we hear of nothing but the American danger," but "we shall not escape this Cossack invasion [of Russia]...only it will emerge in a modern form as agricultural and industrial oppression" (Gollwitzer, 1969, pp. 174–175).

Prescient as those words may have sounded in 1884, by the early part of the twentieth century they were becoming a reality. Vladimir Lenin, the founder of Russian communism, intimated that imperialism represented capitalism's "highest stage" (Gollwitzer, p. 122), and that given capitalism's "inevitable" demise it was communism that would become its imperialist successor. It wasn't until Joseph Stalin, however, that communist *policy* became imperialist. Beginning with the elimination of all legitimately threatening dissent within Russia, Stalin went on to annex territory within Eastern Europe on a massive, and as yet, unprecedented, scale. Following World War II, the so-called Soviet Bloc consisted of the largest part of the old Russian empire, plus several more neighboring states. These included the states of the Union of Soviet Socialist Republics (or USSR)—Estonia, Latvia, Lithuania, Belorussia, Ukraine, Georgia, Armenia, Moldova, Azerbaijan, Kazakhstan, Kyrgyzstan, Turkmenistan, Tajikistan, and Uzbekistan—plus the satellite states of Poland, East Germany, Czechoslovakia, Hungary, Romania, Yugoslavia, and Bulgaria. Furthermore,

Russia formed alliances with communist China and North Korea, as well as parts of Southeast Asia.

The full extent of Stalin's control over the Soviet empire almost defies description. There were repeated purges of opposition leaders, an unprecedented network of secret police, mass seizures of farmable land, mass redistributions of wealth, forced policies of collectivization, and mass abductions, assassinations, and slaughter of those unwilling to conform. By some estimates, from the late 1920s to 1953 (the year of Stalin's death), Stalinist Russia was responsible for the killing of some 11 million of its own citizenry (Snyder, 2011, March).

Like the French Revolution, many of the principles of the 1917 Russian Revolution were liberationist in nature—the defeat of Tsarist tyranny, the equalization of class, the restraint of opulence, the eradication of religious dogma, the support of oppressed minorities, and the provision of health and education for all. But equally striking were the tragic parallels to the French Revolution—reverse tyranny, dogma, and oppression (Service, 2009). These translated into the following Marxist–Leninist principles of state: "the dictatorship of the proletariat [working class]; violence as the midwife of revolutionary transformation; hierarchy; discipline and centralism...; the incontrovertibility of Marxism; and the inevitability of world revolution" (Service, p. 154).

While Lenin mobilized the working class to revolt against the virtually obscene wealth of the Russian nobility, he died before he could fully form and implement his reforms. However, Stalin "resolved" this situation. Not only did he muscle his way into succeeding Lenin as party leader, but also by the late 1920s, he began a campaign of terror that aimed at the "systematic extermination" of all opposition to Central Party control (Service, p. 219). To accomplish this task, Stalin resorted to a variety of both secret and dauntingly open policies of annihilation. Some of these policies involved the NKVD (predecessor to the KGB or Soviet secret police), some involved show trials, and some entailed mass executions. In 1937–1938 alone, it is estimated that some one million to one and one-half million people were killed by firing squad, malnutrition, or severe overwork (p. 222). To be sure, a part of this mass killing stemmed from the threat posed by the "White Army," comprised of peasants, nobles, and Cossacks bent on returning the country to Czarist rule. But this was only a fraction of its agenda; its chief objective was to suppress dissent (Service, 2009).

Who was Stalin and what led to his ascendance as one of the world's most notorious dictators? Stalin was born Iosif Dzhugashvilli in the Russian province of Georgia to parents of modest means. His father was allegedly a "child-beating drunkard who died leaving the family penniless" (p. 196). According to a friend who "knew the family well," Stalin's father beat his son mercilessly, remorselessly, with a kind of brooding, deliberate passion, without pleasure and without any sense of guilt or wrongdoing, for no other purpose than to provide himself with some excitement in an otherwise empty and purposeless existence. The result was inevitable. The boy learned to hate....became hardened by his beatings, and became in the end terrifyingly indifferent to cruelty (Payne cited in Miller, 1990, pp. 63–64).

As a result of these ordeals, Stalin largely raised himself. Although his mother had the wherewithal to enroll him in a seminary where he was provided a substantive religious education, he ultimately rejected it. His proclivities apparently leaned toward modernism, Lenin's revolutionary writings, and violence (p. 196). Stalin allegedly remarked: "To choose one's victims, to prepare one's plans minutely, to slake an implacable vengeance, and then to go to bed...there is nothing sweeter in the world" (Service, pp. 197–8). Stalin also identified with notorious despots of the past, such as Ivan the Terrible and Peter the Great. But in his self-comparison, he was also imperiously critical of them. Of Ivan the Terrible he declared:

> One of Ivan the Terrible's mistakes was to overlook the five great feudal families [who eventually defeated him]. If he had annihilated those five families, there would definitely have been no Time of Troubles. But Ivan the Terrible would execute someone and then spend a long time repenting and praying, God got in his way in this matter. He ought to have been more decisive! (cited in Service, pp. 226–227)

Reportedly, many Russian people loved Stalin, as they did Lenin (p. 199). The cult of Stalin became a mainstay and has coattails right up to the current era. Stalin gave ordinary Russians a renewed pride, though much of it was brutally instilled. He provided a living wage and a basic education to many who were formerly powerless. He also brandished Russia's power in the world (including and notwithstanding its defeat of Hitler). But just as we've seen repeatedly down through history, the case of Stalin is a case of psycho-political convergence: a polarized leader meets a polarized populace and the results are cataclysmic.

This scenario was to reach an apex less than 10 years after Stalin's death in 1953, and following the alleged repudiation of his ideas. By October 1962, Russia's annexation of East Berlin was a public relations disaster. East Berliners, many of them doctors and scientists, were pouring into West Berlin to obtain a higher standard of living, and the Soviet Central Committee (or Presidium), led by Stalin's successor Nikita Krushchev, was becoming increasingly agitated. As a result, the Presidium gave Krushchev a comparatively free hand to bolster Russia's image across the world and, in particular, to impress upon NATO (North Atlantic Treaty Organization) countries that Russia remained a formidable foe. To compound this problem, Russia had long chafed over the U.S. placement of nuclear missiles in nearby Turkey; at a time of rising tension with NATO, this former action only added to their existential angst.

While the Presidium monitored the situation, it was Krushchev who took the bold, and many would say reckless, steps to place Soviet nuclear missiles in Cuba to (in his view) counter American aggression (Service, 2009). While newly appointed communist dictator Fidel Castro's call for Krushchev to bomb American cities was viewed as "madness" by Krushchev, the tension between U.S. and Soviet militaries could not have been higher. Fortunately, cooler heads prevailed and U.S. president John Kennedy pressured Krushchev to remove the Cuban missiles in exchange for a commensurate removal of U.S. missiles in Turkey (Service, p. 374). Although nuclear holocaust was avoided in this world-shaking, ultra-polarizing event, it

came about as close as anything ever has to dooming life as we
know it on this planet.

The Soviet revolution ended formally in August of 1991.
However, the Soviet mentality arguably is still very much alive,
albeit in a much less flagrant form. Russian democratization has
been coupled with continued intimidation of the press,
inflammatory rhetoric, election abuse, violent repression of
dissent, and control of the media (p. 558). When former
intelligence officer and President Vladimir Putin described the
dismantling of the USSR as "the greatest geopolitical catastrophe
of the twentieth century," (p. 548), his policies at the start of the
twenty-first century strayed little from his sentiments. For
example, journalists critical of Putin's administration during the
conflict with the breakaway Moslem republic of Chechnya, were
exposed to "repeated acts of persecution" (p. 556). In 2006,
investigative journalist Anna Politkovskaya, who was critical of
the war, was suspiciously murdered outside of her Moscow
apartment (p. 556); and reporter Vladimir Slivyak, who exposed
the "widespread negligence in the civil nuclear industry," was
"treated as a traitor and subjected to continual harassment" (p.
556). In 2005, Putin placed a compulsory registration
requirement on thousands of civil associations—from charities to
recreational organizations—to bolster centralized oversight.
During that same period, academic textbooks were closely vetted
by the state and authors were compelled to moderate any
criticism of Stalin (p. 557). Finally, in 2007, Putin's handpicked successor, Dmitri Medvedev, was accorded lavish state
resources to defeat opposition candidates, who were either
expelled from the race on technical grounds or deprived of
commensurate media opportunities (p. 559).

While the direction of centralized authority in Russia has yet
to be solidified, it is apparent that for those who resist such
authority there will be numerous barriers to reform.

Imperial Japan

The moment that U.S. Admiral Matthew Perry decided to
"shock" Japan out of its isolation in July of 1853, he could have
hardly anticipated the results—or could he have? Even in that
imperious and self-congratulatory era of American expansion,

perhaps Perry, and U.S. president Millard Fillmore, who authorized the incursion, could have been more circumspect. They could have shown more discretion toward a nation about which the Western industrialized world knew preciously little nor had bothered to substantively investigate. But then again, this type of negligence has not been unique in the annals of self-inflated lives or eras. Tragically, it is routine, with equally routine results.

In that summer of 1853, Perry led a massive flotilla into the Japanese harbor of Tokyo Bay. His mission: to jar the Japanese people into submission and to force their ports into commerce with Western powers (Chang, 1997, p. 21). Although Perry's mission "worked" and the Japanese capitulated to Western interests, the effects on their national consciousness could hardly have been anticipated. The initial blow came from the recognition of U.S. naval superiority, but the core humiliation was internal, the slow burn of a devastated populace. While some Japanese leaders advocated immediate retaliation, others counseled a more strategic course—a course, upon retrospect, that proved harrowingly prophetic. Here's how one of those who represented the strategic route described it:

> As we are not the equals of foreigners in the mechanical arts, let us have intercourse with foreign countries, learn their drill and tactics, and when we have made the [Japanese] nations as united as one family, we shall be able to go abroad and give lands in foreign countries to those who have distinguished themselves in battle; the soldiers will view with one another in displaying their intrepidity, and it will not be too late then to declare war. (cited in Chang, 1997, p. 22)

Fast on the heels of this brewing mentality, a rebel army assembled to overthrow the existing ruler (or Shogun), viewed as primarily responsible for appeasement to the West. The result was a new and more fortified leadership inspired by the Samurai code of "bushido," which required all under its dominion to reenergize and retool. The credo "Revere the Emperor! Expel the barbarians!" and "rich country, strong army" permeated the land (Chang, p. 23). From that point on, during an era known as the "Meiji Restoration," Japan began rapid progress toward modernizing its infrastructure. Additionally, it focused major resources on rejuvenating its military. By the latter part of the nineteenth century, the Meiji government began to recapitulate the strong-arm tactics that had victimized it, just decades earlier, with a series of incursions into Korea and China. Korea was forced to sign a treaty of commerce with Japan, and China acquiesced to a "humiliating" financial arrangement in which Japan was paid for war indemnities and granted substantial regions of land.

Following a series of stinging setbacks at the hands of Western powers at the start of the twentieth century, Japan's animosity toward the West intensified. By the 1920s angry young military leaders urged Japan to avenge the suffering it perceived at the hands of Western colonial powers, such as Russia, England, France, and the United States. Okawa Shumei, a national activist of the time, concluded that "before a new world appears, there must be a deadly fight between the powers of the West and the East....The strongest country in Asia is Japan and the strongest country that represents Europe is America....These two countries are destined to fight" (Chang, p. 27).

Before Shumei's prophetic words would be realized however, Japan turned its sights increasingly on China. Under the increasingly nationalistic leadership of Chiang Kai-shek, Japan's leadership began to grow concerned. Not only did Chiang Kai-shek's nationalism threaten Japan's recent treaty "agreements" with China, it also threatened Japan's sense of entitlement as preeminent ruler of the East. To compound these tensions, Japan appeared to have a very ambivalent relationship toward China. On one hand, it respected China's rich cultural lineage, much of which benefited Japan but, on the other, it resented China's challenge to Japanese supremacy.

As a result of the rising animosity, Japan ramped up its samurai–militant mentality at every turn. Nowhere was this more evident than in the educational system and military academies. In the educational system, "schools operated like miniature military academies," and "some of the teachers were military officers" (Chang, p. 30). Chang reports further that "Teachers...instilled in boys hatred and contempt for the

Chinese people, preparing them for a future invasion of the Chinese mainland" (p. 30). In the military academy, she goes on, "everything in the curriculum was bent toward the goal of perfection and triumph. Above all, the Japanese cadets were to adopt "a will which knows no defeat" (p. 32). Iritani Toshio, an author of the period, summed up the military attitude toward punishment of cadets with wooden rods: "I do not beat you because I hate you. I beat you because I care for you. Do you think I perform these acts with swollen and bloody hands in a state of madness?" (p. 32).

Xenophobia and animosity reached a boiling point when by 1937, Japanese forces, under the command of their "divine" emperor Hirohito, pierced their way into the heartland of China and laid siege to China's former capitol and hallowed historical center, Nanking (now named "Nanjing").

The "rape of Nanking," the subject of many books and films, is now emblazoned on the collective psyche of Chinese victims and Japanese perpetrators alike (Chang, 1997). While this is not the place to detail Japan's role in Nanking, suffice it to say that it is one of the most notorious in all of military history, unsurpassed, perhaps, by any other single wartime incursion (Chang, 1997; Keegan, 1993). Over the course of approximately eight weeks in Nanking, the Japanese military were purported to have slaughtered an estimated 250 to 300 thousand Chinese civilians and military personnel, and to have burned and decimated thousands of homes and civic structures (Chang, 1997, pp. 99–104).

One Japanese soldier, Nagatomi Hakudo, summed up the nature of his and his fellow warriors' actions in the following testament:

> Few know that soldiers impaled babies on bayonets and tossed them still alive into pots of boiling water....They gang-raped women from the ages of twelve to eighty and then killed them when they could no longer satisfy sexual requirements. I beheaded people, starved them to death, burned them, and buried them alive, over two hundred in all. It is terrible that I could turn into an animal and do these

things. There are really no words to explain what I was doing.... (Chang, p. 59)

Following an extensive study of the events leading to and culminating in the atrocities at Nanking and other parts of China, Iris Chang (1997) concluded that three major factors appeared to be at work—each of which is integral to the polarized mind: The first factor she identified was "the transfer of oppression," in which crimes that were perpetrated on the Japanese people in the past became displaced on those whom they subjugated subsequently. To understand this phenomenon, one need only consider the punitive, and some would say sadistic practices, of the Japanese military leadership toward their soldiers, as well as centuries of perceived oppression by both domestic and foreign elites, who held much of the populace in their thrall.

A second factor identified by Chang was "contempt" (or perhaps inverted envy) toward the Chinese people, who were perceived as the sole "rivals" for supremacy in Asia. And a third factor, finally, was religion. This factor pertained directly to the Japanese fixation on emperor worship and the power of collective will. As one Japanese general put it in 1933: "Every single bullet must be charged with the Imperial Way, and every bayonet must have the National Virtue burnt into it" (p. 218).

In conclusion, the Japanese were far from unique in their wholesale emphasis on order, regimentation, and absolutism. As we have seen and shall continue to see, these dimensions follow logically from a brutal familiarity with the unstable. But if we are ever to unhook ourselves from their menace, the distinctive forms that they take and the path of destruction that they leave must starkly and unsparingly be faced.

Nazi Germany

According to Konrad Heiden, author of the introduction to Adolf Hitler's masterwork *Mein Kampf* (1925), early Nazi propaganda stood liberal democracy on its head. Just about everything that many take for granted today, such as the principle of equality, the Nazis repelled from the outset. But they reserved their greatest ire for "freedom-touting" Jews. Paraphrasing Hitler's mentor, Alfred Rosenberg, Heiden (1925/1971) wrote:

[The Jews are] the creators of the modern world, the standard-bearers of the twentieth century and of all that [Rosenberg] and his fellows hated: freedom of speech and press, egalitarian justice, representative government, free access of every citizen to all professions and public services without discrimination of birth, wealth, or religion. (p. xvi)

For Rosenberg, Heiden elaborated,

the belief in human equality [was] a kind of hypnotic spell exercised by world-conquering Judaism with the help of the Christian Churches. Later the Jews invented the mass-seduction of liberal democracy; in the last stage Marxism was their tool. By preaching the principle of human equality, Judaism has attempted to extirpate the feeling of pride from the soul of the Aryan race, to rob them of their leadership. (p. xix)

It was against this background and the effort to "give back" to the Aryan race its "former consciousness of superiority by inculcating the principle that men are *not* equal that *Mein Kampf* was formulated" (p. xix). By comparing his own humiliating past with that of the Germanic people following their defeat in World War I, Hitler contended that not only was rejuvenation possible, it was imperative beyond peoples' wildest imagination.

To give an indication of the timeliness of Hitler's message, consider the following: Post-war Germany was in a shambles— the military was decimated, the leadership was crushed, the Versailles Peace Treaty crippled Germany's economy, and the dreams of a pan-Germanic Europe, echoing Germany's "glorious" racial and ethnic past, was awash (Evans, 2008; Shirer, 1959).

To add to this state of affairs, Alice Miller (1990) elaborated on yet another dark legacy impacting Germany's self-image—its traditional family structure:

I have often compared the structure of Hitler's family to a totalitarian regime in which there is no possibility of recourse against the police state. Hitler's father's exercise of power was the highest authority, from which there was no escape....The boy [Adolf] was never permitted to doubt the rightness of his parents' decisions, for that would have resulted in unbearable torture....[T]he suppression of all the child's needs, indeed of almost every human emotion—was done in the name of a good upbringing. (p. 51)

Miller (1990) goes on to extrapolate Hitler's ordeals to those of his fellow compatriots:

...Hitler's aids accepted his methods without hesitation because for them too this system of coercion and enforced obedience had always been the only right one; they were comfortable with it and never questioned it. When someone has been exposed throughout childhood to nothing but harshness, coldness, coercion, and the rigid wielding of power, as Hitler and his closest followers were, when any sign of softness, tenderness, creativity or vitality is scorned, then the person against whom the violence is directed accepts it as perfectly justified. Children believe they deserve the blows they are given, idealize their persecutors, and later search out objects for projection, displacing their supposed guilt onto other individuals or even a whole people. (pp. 52–53)

It is no wonder then that with this inglorious background, nationalistic groups began to proliferate in Germany, and Hitler's rise to prominence occurred at their very apex. The National Socialist German Workers Party was for many the answer to Germany's woes, and Hitler, by dint of his pluck during World War I, his formidable oratory abilities, and his masterful skills at political manipulation, was a "natural" to lead the movement. To solidify his place as leader, however, Hitler needed more than oratory, and by 1924, during a several-month imprisonment for treason, he set out to document his ideology. The result was his 1925 biography *Mein Kampf* (or "my struggle"), which was also meant as a manifesto for the Nazi cause. And this it assuredly became. Although sales of *Mein Kampf* were modest at first, by 1930, just three years before Hitler came to power, they rose remarkably; and by 1940, the book had sold six million German copies (second only to the Christian Bible)! (Evans, 2008, p. 566; Heider, 1925/1971, p. xix).

Not only did *Mein Kampf* attract a wide following just prior to and during Hitler's reign, it telegraphed just about everything he and his collaborators intended for the world. In addition to suggesting the establishment of world domination by the so-called Aryan (or Germanic) race, the book also intimated the necessity of eradicating Judaism. "The mightiest counterpart to the Aryan," Hitler inveighed, "is represented by the Jew" (p. 300). "Since the Jew," he goes on, "was never in possession of a culture of his own, the foundations of his intellectual work were always provided by others" (p. 301). And in another place he intones: The Jew "is and remains the typical parasite, a sponger who like a noxious bacillus keeps spreading as soon as a favorable medium invites him. And the effect of his existence is also like that of spongers: wherever he appears, the host people die out after a shorter or longer period" (p. 305).

Nazism (or the National Socialist German Worker's Party) began as a labor movement with deep ties to German and Prussian nationalism. Some spokespeople for this nationalistic fervor, such as Guido von List and Jorg Lanz, had a significant affect on Hitler, as well as on several of his key collaborators. Without belaboring the details of this influence, suffice it to say that it not only advocated for a politically resurgent Germany but for a pre-Christian Occultism that ennobled the Germanic race (see The Occult History of the Third Reich, 1991). This spiritually pure and ethnically elevated belief system included Hitler's own belief that he was the "Stark von Oben," or "Strong One From Above" sent by providence to create a "Thousand Year Reich" (Occult History'). The belief system also purportedly influenced Heinrich Himmler, the head of Hitler's secret police (the "SS"), among others that included Alfred Rosenberg and Rudolf Hess (Occult History').

Hence, what began as a thuggish "workers" movement ballooned ultimately into a populist, totalitarian ideology. "You are now the master race here," Ludolf von Alvensleben, adjutant to Heinrich Himmler, told his troops at the start of the blitzkrieg into Poland. "Don't be soft," he elaborated. "Be merciless and clear out everything that is not German and could hinder us in the work of construction" (Evans, 2008, p. 14).

The Nazi obsession with purity, with hygiene, and with social stratification had achieved a new historical height (or depth). When Hitler wrote about the Jews that "His spreading is a typical phenomenon for all parasites," and that "he always seeks a new feeding ground for his race" (p. 305), he set the stage for what Robert Jay Lifton (1986) called the "Nazi biomedical vision" (p. 22). This vision, according to Lifton, was a metaphor for the eradication for all that deviated from the purported Aryan make-up—a total "cleansing," as it were, to make way for the social-Darwinian god-man (that is, Aryan) to rule the earth. All who threatened this cleansing process were conceived of as "cancers," lodged upon the body of the state. Among those seen as cancers were not only Jews but Romanian Gypsies, Slavs, and so-called mental defectives (which included the mentally and emotionally disabled as well as homosexuals) (Evans, 2008).

The fixation on purity and "social hygiene" would seem baffling enough in the mentality of ordinary bureaucrats and military personnel, but it is absolutely stupefying in the mentality of those who are purportedly humanitarian and learned professionals. On this point, Lifton (1986) informs us that "one of the highest ratios" of Nazi Party members in any profession were the medical doctors at 45%; their representation in the SS, for example, was fully seven times that of teachers (p. 34). These doctors and their allied staff oversaw mass sterilization programs at death camps, directed gas chamber selections, conducted bizarre investigations of human toxins, and oversaw the production, administration, and formulation of the gas Zyklon-B, which resulted in countless exterminations.

As if that were not enough, it cannot go unnoticed that fully *eight out of the fifteen* leaders who met at the Wansee conference to deliberate the genocide of the Jewish people were nonmedical *doctors*. Although it stretches credulity to picture any sober adult sitting around a table discussing the most efficient means of liquidating an entire race, it becomes even more unbelievable to consider those who had achieved society's highest educational rank doing just that. To link name, credential, and deed on that fateful January day in 1942, here is a listing of the participants with doctoral degrees:

Dr. Alfred Meyer, Reich Ministry for the Occupied Eastern Territories (PhD in Political Science)

Dr. George Liebbrandt, Reich Ministry for the Occupied Eastern Territories, Permanent Secretary (PhD in Theology, Philosophy, and National Economy)

Dr. Wilhelm Stuckart, Reich Ministry for the Interior (Dr. of Law)

Dr. Roland Freisler, Reich Ministry of Justice (Dr. of Law)

Dr. Josef Bühler, Office of General Government (Poland) (Dr. of Law)

Dr. Karl Schongarth, Commander of the Security Police and the SD for Government General (Dr. of Law)

Dr. Rudolf Lange, Commander of the Security Police and SD for Latvia (Dr. of Law)

Dr. Gerhard Klopfer, Nazi Party Chancellery (Dr. of Law)

(Wannsee Conference, 1942)

The question of how or why Nazism held so many in its thrall has been the subject of countless methodical studies. This is not the place to belabor those studies. However, what can emerge from this brief analysis is that Hitler and his adherents became swept up in a fixation of such ferocity and panic that it overrode any conventional notion of civility. It was a fixation, although perhaps on a comparatively greater scale, that we have seen many times before in this book, and it all appears to converge on one basic problem. This problem will not be seen in the outpouring of patriotic crowds or the grind of military machinery but in the rumbles below, so to speak: in the private expressions of indignation, the paranoid and hate-filled literature, and the desperate living conditions of a brutalized culture.

In short, the problem that cuts beneath simply wounded pride or vengeful sentiment is cosmic *insignificance*. This condition led to two basic effects: inflationary grandiosity to ward off subterranean helplessness, and rigid compulsiveness to ward off residual needs for hypercontrol and management of

risks. The inflationary grandiosity manifested in one of the most
brutal and imperious regimes known to humanity, and the
residual needs for hypercontrol manifested in the obsession with
cleanliness, purity, and religious-like Nazi ritual (see Fromm,
1965). To put it another way, one rarely rids oneself completely
of one's primary sense of insignificance (hyperconstriction);
compensatory grandiosity (e.g., militaristic hyperexpansion)
takes one only so far. Expansion fears such as risk taking and
experimentation remain and can only be assuaged by
compensatory adjustments in the opposite direction. In the case
of Hitler's Germany, this direction took the form of the
obsession with the "other," the purification of the race, and the
preoccupation with "heritage."

To the extent that Hitler as a person and Germany as a
people are understood on the basis of their profound insecurity
with being (identity, cohesion, worth), then, in my view, we have
taken a step toward unveiling their compensatory furor.
Correspondingly, we have taken a step toward addressing
mystery denial in our contemporary age.

Maoist China: Cult and Absolutism

The repugnance toward insignificance has almost incalculable
effects.[5] Between the years of 1933 and 1952, Hitler and Stalin
were responsible for upwards of 40 million deaths (Conquest,
1991; Snyder, 2010). In the East, the Japanese empire accounted
for another 10 to 20 million deaths, and communist China, just
as it was emerging from that tragic victimization, began to
instigate its own grim lineage.

Mao Zedong arose from a poor rural background in China's
Hunan Province (Howard, 1977). He came of age (the late
1800s and early 1900s) at a time when China, too, suffered great
internal and external strife. On the external side, China was
threatened by an increasingly expansionist Japanese empire. On
the internal side, China reeled from two polarizing mentalities—

---

[5]For elaboration on this point, see J. Stephenson's *Poisonous power:
Childhood roots of tyranny*, Diemer Smith, 1998; M.A. Milburn and S.D.
Conrad's *The politics of denial*, MIT Press, 1998; and J. Gilligan's *Violence*,
Vintage, 1997.

the feudal landlords of the countryside and their urban capitalist counterparts, on the one hand, and the rural and urban masses, on the other. Mao and his family were predominantly from the latter class, and much that followed in his life was a reflection of that disposition.

Mao's father was allegedly "stern" and "autocratic" (Howard, 1977, p. 30). Much like the profile of Hitler and Stalin's fathers, he appeared to have become intractably embittered by life circumstances, and though achieving a modest income, he placed great emphasis on power, status, and regimentation. This emphasis enabled very little place for self-development in Mao's household, although Mao's mother provided an ambivalent counterbalance (Howard, 1977). "There were two 'parties' in the family," Mao elaborated (p. 31). "One was my father, the Ruling Power. The opposition was myself, my mother, my brother, and sometimes even a laborer. [But] my mother...criticized any overt display of emotion and attempts at open rebellion against the Ruling Power. She said it was not the Chinese way" (p. 31).

Yet like so many other evolving autocrats that we have seen in this volume Mao was not easily coerced as a youth. He learned many lessons about cruelty in his relationship with his father—both as a coercive influence and instigator of rebellion. When Mao was "about ten, his father cursed him one day and was going to beat him for his 'laziness' and 'uselessness.' [Mao] rushed out in a fury and, saying he would drown himself in a pond, demanded that his father withdraw his threats. He did so, and [Mao] too apologized." Mao took this story as an important lesson about power. He recounted: "When I defended my rights by open rebellion my father relented, but when I remained meek and submissive he only cursed and beat me the more" (pp. 31–32).

Mao learned parallel lessons in school. "His repertoire included many forms of corporeal punishment such as flogging, beating on the palm, head, feet and thighs and 'incense kneeling'" (p. 32). Incense kneeling was a particularly painful form of punishment whereby the student perpetrator would be forced to kneel on a hard surface like gravel for the entire length of time it would take for an incense candle to burn out. Mao's reaction to these types of procedures was similar to those he exhibited with his father—he made every effort to avoid them. For example, after a particularly quarrelsome encounter with his teacher, he ran away from school for a sufficient length of time to cool off the tempers of both his teacher and his father (p. 33).

These cooling-off periods, however, were apparently short-lived. Following a prolonged period of battling with his father and repelled by the work he was required to carry out for him, Mao, at just 13 years old, ran away from home. During this period, 1906, a great flood and then famine swept through Hunan province and Mao took up temporary residence with a nearby neighbor. Mao observed that the rich farmers in the area refused to help the poor, whom they humiliated even further by selling their grains to city dwellers. The poor farmers, in the meantime, became so desperate and infuriated that they decided to steal grains from the landowners. After about six months, Mao returned home to work for his father and found that the poor farmers had stolen from his father's supply as well. Yet Mao was of two minds about these events; he sympathized neither with his father and the rich nor with the tactics of the poor farmers.

At 16, Mao enrolled in a "modern" school that taught him a diversified curriculum from the classics to essay writing to the natural sciences, history, and geography. Like young Napoleon at his elite French academy, Mao was comparatively poor for his peer group and, according to his own testimony, many of the wealthier students "despised" him (Howard, 1977, p. 35).

In time, Mao worked his way toward becoming a young revolutionary. After a sustained period living in Peking (now Beijing), Mao immersed himself in communist literature and began to help organize labor strikes. He became increasingly identified as a champion of the masses against the elite rulers and wrote compelling revolutionary essays in a language the masses could easily understand. Here is a sample from the *Hsiang River Review*, which was subsequently banned by local authorities:

What is the greatest question in the world? The greatest question is that of getting food to eat. What is the greatest force? The greatest force is that of the union of the popular masses....If we do not act, who will act? If we do not rise up and fight, who will rise up and fight?....The great union of the Chinese people must be achieved.... (cited in Howard, pp. 47–48)

Mao's discoveries about action in the face of cruelty, and the need, in his view, to reverse the hierarchy of power, both in his family and the society at large, took a decisive turn following Japan's invasion of China in the late 1930s. During this time, Mao managed to help unify and hence mobilize the vast citizenry that had been marginalized by centuries of feudal rule. By stressing both internal as well as external liberation from oppressive elites, Mao found a platform that shook the foundations of his society, as well as the world, for decades to come.

Following the termination of WWII and the success of Mao's communist insurrection against the reigning rule of Chiang Kai-shek in 1948, Mao's ascendance to power was marked by two landmark cultural movements—The Great Leap Forward (1958–1962) and the Cultural Revolution (1966–1975). With these movements, Mao's ideals about reversal of elitist power mongering were pressed toward fruition. Although he had some democratic beliefs mixed in with his institution of proletariat reforms, they were jarringly constrained. For example, he professed a belief in diversity of opinion— something he called the "contradictions among the people" (Howard, p. 273), but he also believed that diversity had its strict limits. During the early '50s when Mao and the Chinese Communist Party (CCP) implemented the land reform movement, tenants were encouraged to admonish their landlords in a public spectacle of "rehabilitation" called a "struggle session." Struggle sessions allegedly promoted free speech, but they were prearranged to thwart it. Landlords, for example, were baited to give their side of the story in these sessions, but when they did they were summarily humiliated and executed—approximately two to five million in total (http://en.wikipedia.org/wiki/Struggle_session). During the "Hundred Flowers" campaign just prior to the Great Leap Forward, Mao and the CCP began a policy of supporting free speech, which even included criticism of the communist government. The campaign turned out to be a "disaster" however, as many more people than expected turned out to criticize the regime. When this happened, Mao and the Party were appalled and allegedly had millions of these critics executed (Chang & Halliday, 2005, p. 410). Struggle sessions were also frequently used during the Cultural Revolution to "reeducate" Party elites, artistic and literary intellectuals, and political dissenters (Chang & Halliday, 2005).

Mao characterized his revolutionary government as a "democratic dictatorship," in which the peasants or masses were allegedly emancipated, and the ruling classes (or counter-revolutionaries) were "compel[led]...to transform themselves into new people through labor" (p. 252). But the facts belie Mao's stated intent. During the Great Leap Forward, for example, immense rhetoric was focused on industrializing China's infrastructure for the benefit of all its people, but many of the actual resources put to that commitment were squandered on mismanagement and diversion from the neediest populations. When a famine occurred in 1959, Mao and the Chinese leadership appeared to favor workers in the cities and robust exports more than peasant farmers who perished by the millions (Mishra, 2010, Dec 20). In response to this debacle, Mao quipped: "When there is not enough to eat, people starve to death. It is better to let half of the people die so that the other half can eat their fill" (Mishra, p. 127). During the Cultural Revolution, Mao's intent was to purge his Party of capitalist-leaning elites, but he ended up, some say vengefully, persecuting and annihilating huge swaths of the country's core intellectual and cultural leadership.

By the time of Mao's death in 1976, an entire nation reeled from his depredations. By some estimates, Mao and his regime were responsible for up to 70 million deaths (Mishra, p. 126). While Mao did make good on his promise to transform China from a puppet of Japanese and Western imperialism into a rising superpower, the price for his tactics cannot be ignored. Mao drew on the lessons of his personal emergence from abuse to uplift his nation, but the blindness of his (and their) ascent cast a pall of incalculable sorrow. This sorrow could be seen in policies that initially courted openness but ultimately countenanced absolutism, that professed egalitarianism but that advantaged the despotic, and that lionized education but handcuffed its champions. So great were Mao and his compatriot's desperation for significance that during the Great Leap Forward they tolerated whole sectors of starvation so that the appearance of invincibility could be maintained. So great were Mao and his compatriots' desire for super status that when doubters emerged during the Cultural Revolution they were publicly debased.

In addition, fears of becoming *too* significant, of standing out and retriggering fears of unmanageable power and responsibility also played a role in the Maoist regime. For all their bravado, Mao and his allies lived an intellectually and emotionally impoverished life. They held dissenters at bay, adhered rigidly to doctrine, and isolated themselves from the larger world. These maneuvers paralleled precisely the coping mechanisms that Mao (and many others) had to learn growing up, and while fending off imperial adversaries.

The result, however, was that Mao upended tradition to the point where the replacement looked viler than its predecessor, and the hope for new life, dimmer than the outlook it originally opposed. This, again, is the legacy of ontological panic and the absolutism, coercion, and imperiousness that so often follow.

Chapter 3

Expanding the Expansionism

As we have seen, the successors to mystery denial have affected enormous regions of the contemporary globe. They have committed untold atrocities and they have altered the course of human evolution. Due largely to the advancement of technology however, these developments pale in comparison to present influences on humanity. Some of these influences appear benign, some welcome, and others (too many others) downright horrifying. We now consider the successor that is at the hub of these influences, the colossus of the emerging epoch, the United States of America.

The Expansionist Shadow of America

Arguably, the United States of America is the most successful democracy in history; it is also the most expansionist. Presently, we consider two key bases for this expansionism—racism and mercantilism—which link intimately to the contemporary world.

Colonial Beginnings

To understand America's expansionist lineage, it is instructive to recap the notes of Columbus. The "natives" of the Bahama Islands, he recorded in 1492 upon "discovering" the Americas, "have no iron" and their "spears are made of Cane" (Zinn, 2003, p. 1). A few lines later he described the opportunity this state of affairs presented for exploitation: The natives "would make fine servants," he opined. "With fifty men we could subjugate them all and make them do whatever we want" (p. 1). In his report to the court in Madrid upon his return, Columbus seemed to delight in the innocence of the native "Indians." He related that they "are so naïve and so free with their possessions that no one who has not witnessed them believe it. When you ask for something they have, they never say no. To the contrary, they offer to share with anyone" (p. 3). In his next voyage, Columbus assured his creditors that he would reward them with "as much gold as they need...and as many slaves as they ask" (p. 4).

Soon after his initial voyage, Columbus took ten natives to "display" before the court of King Ferdinand and Queen Isabella. "Two years later he shipped off five hundred West Indian natives as slaves; nearly all of them died of disease" (Nabokov, 1978, p. 19). By 1550, Zinn reports, the Bahamian natives had been decimated by the Spanish invaders, and of the 250,000 natives on nearby Haiti, only 500 remained (p. 5).

By the time of the English settlements in Jamestown Virginia in the early 1600s, the pattern of White dominance over native peoples had been firmly set. Although the settlers established colonies on Indian land, relied on them for food during periods of starvation, and learned from them about how to cultivate the land, their sense of entitlement seemed to know few bounds. When an Indian stole a small silver cup from one of the earliest settlements, the leader of the settlement, Richard Grenville, "sacked and burned the whole Indian village" (p. 12). When, some years later, the governor of Jamestown asked the chief of the surrounding confederation of tribes to return runaway settlers who had sought haven with the Indians during a period of starvation, and was met with "prowde and disdaynefull Answers," he authorized a contingent of soldiers to burn and terrorize an Indian settlement. The result of this operation was that fifteen or sixteen Indians were killed, houses were burned, and the queen of the village was taken with her children and killed (p.12).

This pattern of meeting comparatively modest infractions with all-out butchery was repeated countless times over the subsequent 300 years of White incursion into the Americas. Compounding this sense of entitlement appeared to be the psychological factor of envy. White settlers, who had remarkable skills in the production of technologies, from transport to weaponry, proved almost pitiable when it came to adaptation to the wilderness. The Indians by comparison were master hunters, planters, scouts, and foragers, and they somehow seemed to harmonize with their environments. The historian Edmund Morgan characterized the settlers' frustration as follows:

If you were a colonist, you knew that your technology was
superior to the Indians'. You knew that you were civilized
and they were savages.... But your superior technology had
proved insufficient to extract anything. The Indians, keeping
to themselves, laughed at your superior methods and lived
from the land more abundantly and with less labor than you
did....And when your own people started deserting in order
to live with them, it was too much....So you killed the
Indians, tortured them, burned their villages, burned their
cornfields. It proved your superiority, in spite of your
failures. And you gave similar treatment to any of your own
people who succumbed to their savage ways of life. But you
still did not grow corn.... (cited in Zinn, p. 25)

The drive to be "right," to dominate the "inferior," and to
expand territory seemed almost insatiable among some White
colonists, especially the elite. Perhaps this zeal was fueled in
part by the degradation they themselves had experienced and
thus needed to displace on others, such as Indians and later West
African slaves. But it also appeared to be driven by desperation
for capital and the things that capital represented in the
seventeenth century world—power, autonomy, and control—
everything these settlers lacked in their lands of origin.

F. Scott Fitzgerald's *Great Gatsby* is an archetypal depiction
of this desperate pattern of acquisitiveness among American
forebears. Gatsby, like the earliest Americans (Columbus
included) sought everything he could not get in his deprived
station as an underling, a servant of the aristocracy, and a pauper.
But also like the earliest Americans he felt himself to be "free,"
untethered and unobliged, to pursue his lofty dreams. As the
novel implies, this thirst for personal expansion—no matter what
the cost—has been both the boon and bane of the American
character. And its gravest effects have been on race.

In the winter of 1607, half of the new colonists at Jamestown
succumbed to starvation and disease. Without the help of their
Indian neighbors, called the Powhatan confederacy, their entire
colony may have been decimated. In the proceeding call for
friendship following the blight, King Powhatan warns of a
dangerous worsening of relations:

Why should you take by force that from us which you can
have by love?   Why should you destroy us, who have
provided you with food?   What can you get by war?   We can
hide our provisions and fly into the woods; and then you
must consequently famish by wrongdoing your friends.
What is the cause of your jealousy?   You see us unarmed,
and willing to supply your wants, if you will come in a
friendly manner, and not with swords and guns, as to invade
an enemy....Therefore [I] exhort you to peaceable councils;
and above all, I insist that the guns and swords, the cause of
all our jealousy and uneasiness, be removed and sent away.
(Nabokov, 1978, pp. 72–73)

By 1622, the abuses Powhatan warned against intensified to
the point where the Powhatan community exploded in violence
against the colonists, killing 350 of them.   In turn, this was the
pretext for all-out war against the Indians.   By the outset of the
twentieth century, nine tenths of the original 10 million Indians
of North America had either been wiped out by the disease or
weaponry associated with their White European counterparts
(Zinn, 2003, p. 16).

Howard Zinn observed in his "People's History of America"
that, "There is not a country in world history in which racism has
been more important, for so long a time, as in the United States"
(p. 23).   Not only was this point driven home by some of the
most notorious Indian haters among colonists, but it also
apparently included some of America's most distinguished
statesmen.   For example, no less than President George
Washington wrote that both "wolves and Indians were 'beasts of
prey, tho' they differ in shape'" (Berreby, 2011, p. 19).

If America's devaluation and virtual genocide of its native
population was the limit of its bigotry, this would be tragic
enough.   The problem, however, is that this bigotry did not stop
at its own shores.

Slavery
The enslavement of black Africans did not begin with America.
Indeed, there was a history of such slavery within Africa itself.
However, according to Zinn (2003), there were two elements
"that made American slavery the most cruel form of slavery in

history: the frenzy for limitless profit that comes from capitalist agriculture; [and] the reduction of the slave to less than human status by the use of racial hatred, with that relentless clarity based on color, where white was master, black was slave" (p. 28). Zinn quotes an observer of a seventeenth century slave vessel, John Barbot, to elaborate the conditions such ships afforded its human cargo:

> The height, sometimes between decks, was only eighteen inches, so that the unfortunate human beings could not turn around, or even on their sides, the elevation being less than the breadth of their shoulders; and here they are usually chained to the decks by the neck and legs. In such a place the sense of misery and suffocation is so great, that the Negroes…are driven to frenzy. (cited in Zinn, 2003, p. 29)

Although it might be expected that religious institutions, such as the Catholic Church, would inveigh against such barbarian treatments (and indeed they did in exceptional instances), in many cases they did the opposite, and appeased the perpetrators.   In 1610, a Catholic priest from the Americas named Father Sandoval wrote to a church functionary in Europe to inquire about the legality of slavery, and he received the following reply on March 12, 1610:

> Your Reverence writes me that you would like to know whether Negroes who are sent to your ports have been legally captured.   To this I reply that I think Your Reverence should have no scruples on this point, because this is a matter which has been questioned by the Board of Conscience in Lisbon and all its members are learned and conscientious men.   Nor did the bishops who were in Sao Thome, Cape Verde…all learned and virtuous men—find fault with it. (Zinn, p. 29)

Just how deep the white aversion for blackness ran was illustrated by the associations, including linguistic associations, to the term "black." According to the Oxford English Dictionary, prior to 1600 black was associated with "dirt; soiled, dirty, foul" (Zinn, p. 31). "It may be," according to Zinn, that "in the absence of any other overriding factor, darkness and blackness associated with night and unknown..." (p. 31). These associations, I would add, may have been especially anxiety provoking for white colonizers, who knew little about forested and uncultivated lands. In any case, the presence of brown or black skin assuredly elicited fear in many white colonizers, and this fear, coupled with mercantile zeal, made for a harrowing brew.

In the colony of Virginia, for example, a law was passed in 1629 banishing "any white man or woman being free who shall intermarry with a negro, mulatoo [sic], or Indian man or woman bond or free" (p. 31). In the early 1700s, slave overseers in some of the colonies were permitted to whip, burn, mutilate, and even kill their charges for rebellious behavior such as running away (Zinn, p. 34). The Virginia Code of 1705 allowed for slave dismemberment as a punishment for certain serious crimes, and in 1723 Maryland passed a law "providing for cutting off the ears of blacks who struck whites" (p. 35). Further, this law mandated that for more serious crimes "slaves should be hanged" and their bodies "quartered and exposed" (p. 35).

By 1800, "10 to 15 million blacks had been transported as slaves to the Americas, representing perhaps one-third of those originally seized in Africa" (p. 29). This means that 30 to 45 million black slaves were unaccounted for (or may well have perished) during their journey from Africa to the Americas between the 1500s and 1800. Add to that the total number of slaves who died from poor conditions and/or maltreatment by their masters in the Americas, and the totality of the calamity is staggering. Despite these grim statistics, many, especially elite figures in the U.S. government, acted as if slavery was a necessary condition of the economy. Not only did Thomas Jefferson, who owned hundreds of slaves, appear to hold this view, but also leaders such as James Madison, who "told a British visitor shortly after the American Revolution that he could make $257 on every Negro in a year, and spend only $12 or $13 on his keep" (Zinn, p. 33). It wasn't until Abraham Lincoln that a major white politician took a decisive stand against slavery, but even then, it was fraught with equivocation, at least in its early formulation. While during his 1858 campaign in Chicago Lincoln conveyed the need to "discard all this quibbling about this man and the other man, this race and that race and the other race being inferior" (p. 188), two months later at a campaign stop in southern Illinois he proclaimed:

> I am not, nor ever have been, in favor of bringing about in any way the social and political equality of the white and black race....I am not, nor ever have been, in favor of making voters or jurors of negroes, nor of qualifying them to hold office, nor to intermarry with white people....[T]here must be the position of superior and inferior, and I as much as any other man am in favor of having the superior position assigned to the white race. (Zinn, p. 188)

Whichever stance one takes toward Lincoln's abolitionist or nonabolitionist leanings, it does appear evident that the liberation of African Americans was not his top priority, whereas ensuring a stable and unified republic was. In an 1862 letter to Horace Greely, editor of the *New York Tribune*, Lincoln wrote: "Dear Sir....I have not meant to leave any one in doubt....My paramount object in this struggle is to save the Union, and not either to save or destroy Slavery. If I could save the Union without freeing any slave, I would do it..." (p. 191). At the same time, Lincoln concluded the letter by distinguishing between his "official duty," which was to ensure a unified republic (regardless of the slavery question), and his "oft-expressed personal wish that all men, everywhere, could be free" (p. 191).

The fact that Lincoln felt obliged to distinguish between his official duty as a governmental agent and his personal wishes speaks volumes about the political ethos of late nineteenth century America. Although blacks were permitted token gains in civic and political affairs immediately following their emancipation in 1865, these were quickly quashed by a series of polarizing legal decrees. Such decrees favored states' rights in a blistering attack on black voting rights, opportunities for an equal and integrated education, and opportunities for civic and social advancement (Zinn, 2003). Ex-slave Thomas Hall testified that although

Lincoln got the praise for freeing us...did he do it? He gave us freedom without giving us any chance to live to ourselves and we still had to depend on the southern white man for work, food, and clothing, and he held us out of necessity and want in a state of servitude but little better than slavery. (pp. 197-198).

And the American north was by no means exempt from these indictments—even with its self-professed "tolerance" (Zinn, 2003).

Mercantile Lust
Paralleling and in many ways fueling the dehumanizing policies against blacks and Indians, America harbored another "war" against its inhabitants. This was the war to establish wealth and material possessions at all costs, to fight centralization and regulatory authority at all costs, and to be "free," however and whenever this freedom could be achieved. Partly as a counter-reaction to their European oppressors, many Americans sought aggressively to own large swaths of land, develop lucrative business schemes, and cultivate large commercial enterprises. These endeavors proved wildly successful by some measures: they enriched the farmable land, built up sheltering infrastructure, and inspired innovative production. But they also crushed people. They neglected the poor, the feeble, the people of color, women, and the socially dissident. The emphasis for many of these hard-driving achievers was on freedom, autonomy, and willfulness, but rarely on equality, community, and multicultural respect (Zinn, 2003). Hence, the war on class, on the ability of an individual to "achieve" in the strict terms defined by the achievers in power, became a critical component of the war on Native Americans and blacks. It also became a critical component of the war on the poor and working class, and ultimately, on the regulatory power of government. In a very real sense, then, the entrepreneurial elites of America sought a social Darwinist world, where "every man for himself," "the sky's the limit," and "only the strong survive" became the new watchwords of the Republic.

During the late nineteenth and early twentieth centuries, the twin legacies of racism and mercantilism began to take on new and beguiling forms. Although these forms were not as directly barbarous as their predecessors, their consequences were equally dire. For example, as a result of the monopolistic excesses of top railway and oil executives at the end of the nineteenth century, working class whites—as well as blacks—suffered enormous inequities in income, hours worked, and job safety, as compared to their managerial counterparts (Zinn, 2003). Books like Upton Sinclair's *The Jungle*, exposed the inequities of big business, in this case the meatpacking industry, to millions, and also highlighted the plight of child laborers who toiled in dangerous industries for negligible pay. The power of executives such as John D. Rockefeller, Andrew Carnegie, and Andrew Mellon to impact the domestic—as well as foreign—policies of the United States was alarming, and exercised a corrosive effect on governance. It was the convergence of these influences that led to lax trade and labor laws, anemic tax policies, and entries into foreign wars (Zinn, 2003). Drawing upon the religious and political ideology of "manifest destiny," America evolved an attitude of divine justification for all of its important actions, at whatever cost. In 1896, even the president of the United States, William McKinley, drew the connection between national and financial "glory:"

> this year, he proclaimed, is going to be a year of patriotism and devotion to country. I am glad to know that the people in every part of the country mean to be devoted to one flag, the glorious Stars and Stripes; that the people of this country mean to maintain the financial honor of the country as sacredly as they maintain the honor of the flag. (p. 295)

One year later, President Theodore Roosevelt wrote to a friend: "In strict confidence...I should welcome almost any war, for I think this country needs one" (p. 296).

While there were, of course, resistances to these autocratic trends, the proponents of these movements often paid dearly for their protestations. One result was a series of race and labor riots that almost invariably ended in capitulation to the ruling elites

(Zinn, 2003). As early as 1829, a printer and editor of the *Working Man's Advocate*, George Henry Evans, declared:

> The laws for levying taxes are...operating most oppressively on one class of society....The laws for private incorporation are partial...favoring one class of society to the expense of the other....The laws...have deprived nine tenths of the members of the body politics, who are not wealthy, of the equal means to enjoy "life, liberty, and the pursuit of happiness."....The lien law in favor of the landlords against tenants...is one illustration among innumerable others. (p. 222).

By the 1870s, Joseph Dacus, the editor of the St. Louis *Republican*, reported that "strikes" all over the country "were occurring almost every hour. The great State of Pennsylvania was in an uproar; New Jersey was afflicted by a paralyzing dread; New York was mustering an army of militia; Ohio was shaken from Lake Erie to the Ohio River...." (p. 246). While many were killed and wounded during these strikes, major progress on the consolidation of unions and improved working conditions was not established until the 1940s when the Roosevelt Administration instituted landmark reforms. By the same token, major improvement in the working conditions for minorities, especially blacks, was not realized until landmark reforms in the 1950s and 1960s, and in the wake of harrowing social and civil unrest. The attitude of many during the nineteenth and even twentieth and twenty-first centuries was summed up by a late nineteenth century graduate of Yale Law School, founder of Temple University, minister Russell Conwell, who gave lectures based on his best-selling books. One lecture, called "Acres of Diamonds" proceeded as follows:

> I say that you ought to get rich, and it is your duty to get rich....The men who get rich may be the most honest men you find in the community. Let me say here clearly ...ninety-eight out of one hundred of the rich men of America are honest. That is why they are rich. That is why they are trusted with money. That is why they carry on great enterprises and find plenty of people to work with them. It is because they are honest men...sympathize with the poor, but

the number of poor who are to be sympathized with is very small. To sympathize with a man whom God has punished for his sins...is to do wrong....let us remember there is not a poor person in the United States who was not made poor by his own shortcomings... (Zinn, p. 262)

The insatiable drive for capital, it should be noted, was not confined to the elites of right wing or corporate politics. Some of the greatest leaders on the left, such as Teamsters magnate Jimmy Hoffa, were equally culpable. Hoffa rose from the obscurity of a day laborer in the 1930s to become one of the most potent union organizers and working class heroes in U.S. history. He helped to convert the Teamsters, an anemic union comprised of about 75,000 steel and auto laborers in the 1930s, into a blockbuster organization of 1.5 million by the 1960s and 1970s (http://en.wikipedia.org/wiki/Jimmy_Hoffa). At the same time that he fought heroically for the working person, however, Hoffa also succumbed to kickbacks, extortion, and egregious pacts with organized crime. In 1964, he was convicted of siphoning millions in union pension funds to notorious mobsters. Following a lengthy jail term and subsequent attempt to regain his power, he was allegedly assassinated by those same conspirators with whom he shared the pension funds. Hoffa is a case example of the way that financial lust (and by implication a sense of personal insignificance) can twist even the most anti-capitalist reformers. Although the influence of such "reformers" is miniscule in comparison to the financial and corporate titans they challenge, it is nevertheless instructive in a materialist-driven, consumer-obsessed society.

Globalism

Paralleling their thirst for financial expansion, American companies and political leaders also hungered for territorial conquest. In the nineteenth century alone, troops were deployed to "protect American interests" in Argentina (1852–53), Nicaragua (1853), Japan (1853–54), Nicaragua again (1854), Uruguay (1855), China (1859), Angola, Portuguese West Africa (1860), Hawaii (1893), and Nicaragua again (1894). Following a foiled attempt by the Dole Pineapple company, principally led by the Dole family, to set up their own government in Hawaii in

1893, President Theodore Roosevelt reportedly lamented that this failure "was a crime against white civilization." He later noted that "all the great and masterful races have been fighting races" and that "No triumph of peace is quite so great as the supreme triumph of war" (Zinn, p. 300).

All of which led the germinal American philosopher William James to decry: Roosevelt "gushes over war as the ideal condition of human society, for the manly strenuousness which it involves, and treats peace as a condition of blubber like and swollen ignobility, fit only for huckstering weaklings, dwelling in gray twilight and heedless of the higher life..." (Zinn, p. 300).

Even at the height of World War II, some U.S. companies continued to invest in fascist regimes to expand their profit margins. A case in point is Thomas Watson's oversight of IBM. According to recently released documents, Watson, the CEO at the time, actually contracted with Hitler to provide IBM computer technologies to plan and design Nazi death camps (Black, 2002/2012). One of his overriding motives for this abomination, according to investigative journalist Edwin Black, was his "one percent commission on all Nazi business profits" (Black, p. 3).

By the middle of the twentieth century, and following its heroic victories in World Wars I and II, America's yen for expansion took new and subtler turns. While Wisconsin Senator Joseph McCarthy spearheaded hearings into alleged communist infiltration of the U.S. government, leaders in the business and financial worlds began to foment grand designs to open commercial markets. In 1953, in the wake of the democratically elected leader of Iran's decision to nationalize the country's oil supplies, first Great Britain and then the United States became increasingly fearful that their own national interests would be imperiled. Not only did both countries have major commercial interests in Iran's oil, they also bristled at the prospect of growing communist influence at the highest levels of Iran's government (Zinn, 2003). As a result, a decision was made by the Eisenhower administration to back a coup d'etat against Iran's newly elected leader, Mossadegh, and help to install the son of the former dictator of that country, the so-called Shah of Iran. This action proved ill begotten when 26 years later, a fundamentalist Islamic leader, Ayatollah Khomeini, who inspired generations of anti-U.S. sentiment, overthrew the Shah. In 1953, at the behest of the United Fruit Company of Guatemala, the CIA assisted a mercenary invasion force to crush another democratically elected leader, Jacobo Arbenez. Arbenez's apparent crime was to expropriate land owned by United Fruit Company and to offer compensation for the action that was deemed "unacceptable" (Zinn, p. 439). The leader who replaced Arbenez, Colonel Carlos Castillo, not only gave the land back to United Fruit but eliminated "the tax on interest and dividends to foreign investors, eliminated the secret ballot, and jailed thousands of political critics" (p. 439). In 1961, President Kennedy and the CIA attempted to overthrow Fidel Castro at the Bay of Pigs. This insurrection not only failed dismally but sowed the seeds of hate and distrust. Within a year and a half, Castro helped to foment the so-called Cuban Missile Crisis—one of the most notorious nuclear confrontations in world history.

In 1973, another CIA-backed operation with the "collusion" of Secretary of State Henry Kissinger supported a vicious dictator, Auguste Pinochet, in his overthrow of the democratically elected president of Chile, Salvadore Allende. When the American Ambassador to Chile, David Popper, suggested in 1974 that the Chilean Junta (which was also backed by the International Telephone and Telegraph company) had violated human rights, Kissinger allegedly replied, "Tell Popper to cut out the political science lectures" (p. 554).

During the same time period, a neo-conservative academic movement, led by Nobel prize-winning political economist Milton Friedman at the University of Chicago, was beginning to test out a theory of the global domination of free-market economies. Dubbed by journalist Naomi Klein (2007) as "the shock doctrine," this theory held that akin to individuals, states, too, could be traumatized, and that such trauma (for example, a natural or political calamity) would induce states to become reliant on free-market "remedies" for their recovery. Pinochet's overthrow of Allende's regime fit this bill exquisitely, according to Klein, and made sense of the transition advocated by Pinochet from a state-controlled to a commercially controlled economy. It also made sense of Friedman's alleged support of Pinochet's regime, and the help he and his colleagues provided to guide Pinochet toward commercial dependence on large domestic and U.S. firms (Klein, 2007). After 16 years of repressive rule, Pinochet was said to have been responsible for the disappearance or deaths of up to 3,200 citizens, and the torture of as many as 30,000 (http://en.wikipedia.org/wiki/Augusto_Pinochet).

There were more CIA-supported wars, coups, and acts of terror in South Korea (1950), Vietnam (1966), and Argentina (1975), but this activity may have reached its zenith in 2003 with the advent of the second Iraq war and the purposeful manipulation of CIA data by the newly installed Bush administration (Zinn, 2003). In this most infamous example of U.S. supported acts of preemptive aggression in the wake of the terrorist attacks of 9/11/2001, intelligence that was weakly supported, namely Iraq's possession of weapons of mass destruction, was exaggerated. Knowingly dubious about the validity of his data, Secretary of State Colin Powell straightforwardly testified to a U.N. hearing that it was likely that the leader of Iraq, Saddam Hussein, possessed the means to create a nuclear weapon. This data was later found to have been based on false testimony from unreliable informants (Woodward, 2006).

Backlashes Within Backlashes: The New Multi-Polar Reality
The full story of U.S. polarization is the perpetuation of new and more dizzying counter-polarizations. These counter-polarizations have tended to converge on communist backlashes against capitalism (e.g., Cuba, Viet Nam), but they are by no means confined to this dynamic. There are now backlashes (and counter-backlashes) not only against classism and racism, but against secularism, intellectualism, and mercantilism (see Bishop, 2008). By the fall of the Soviet empire in 1991, polarizations and counter-polarizations began to crop up all over the world. Some of these cycles stemmed from ancient blood feuds dating back to feudal and even pre-feudal societies (e.g., Serbia and Albania); however, many of them arose in the wake of Western expansionism during the last two centuries, and the United States, often clandestinely, played a central role.

Beginning with U.S. Admiral Perry's nineteenth century invasion of Japan, for example, Eastern powers such as Japan, China, and Indonesia drew on anti-imperialist resentment to foment their own imperialistic designs. Following U.S. incursions into Latin America, rebel insurgents—such as those in Nicaragua, El Salvador, Cuba, and Argentina—redoubled their efforts to repel capitalist-friendly regimes.

But it is the story in the Middle East that bears particular scrutiny; for it is this story that epitomizes the folly of perceiving the world through one mystery-denying lens. Beginning with the Allied division of spoils following World War I, the entire Middle East was "restructured." Not only did victorious Western allies, such as England, France, and the United States impose artificial borders, from Saudi Arabia to Jordan, Israel to Syria, and Iran to Iraq, but in many cases they occupied or ruled over those territories through military proxy. As previously indicated, Iran was a textbook example of how a dominant U.S. and Western commercialization policy led to equally menacing reversions to theocracy and nationalism. The radicalization in Egypt (under the nationalism of Gamal Nasser), Pakistan (under an Islamic oligarchy), and Iraq (under the militant rule of Saddam Hussein) followed similar patterns.

The role of the United States in fomenting a pattern of pan-Islamic resentment of the state of Israel also cannot be overlooked. Without belaboring this knotty and seemingly intractable situation, suffice it to say that U.S. interests in Israel appeared to be both humanitarian and mercantile. Following the formation of the state of Israel in 1948, the U.S. had abounding moral motivation to support a populace that lost six million of its constituents to the Nazis in World War II, and that suffered from centuries of persecution in the Diaspora of Europe. At the same time, U.S. investment in a stable, strong, and commercially viable ally in the Mid-East could not be overstated, and this investment was not well received by Israel's rankled adversaries. Palestinians, in particular resented the U.S. role in building Israel's arms and infrastructure, while neglecting Palestinian needs for resettlement and recompense. Jordan resented the neglect of displaced Palestinian refugees within its own borders, and Egypt and Syria resented the U.S.-supported military

superiority of Israel to the detriment of their own visions of
sovereignty.

Following the Six-Day War in 1967, in which Israel was
roundly attacked by but ultimately triumphed over her Arab
neighbors, U.S. interests in the country multiplied (Finkelstein,
2000). A part of this increase was clearly attributable to the
sympathy many in the United States felt for Israel's (repeated)
victimization at the hands of a vengeful majority; however,
another part of this concern appeared to be just as clearly
militaristic, expansionist, and commercial (Finkelstein, 2000).
Lucy Dawidowicz, who was an outspoken critic of Israel's
treatment of Palestinians before the Six-Day War, summed up
the sentiment of many following the war when she stated flatly
that the new Israel is "the corporate paradigm for the ideal image
of the Jew in the modern world" (p. 22). It was also at this point
that, despite initial misgivings, the government of Israel
ultimately authorized settlements beyond its original borders.
This authorization has haunted the region's politics ever since.

From 1948 to 1950, a religiously observant Egyptian scholar
named Sayyid Qutb visited the United States to discover more
about the country that appeared to dominate his own region, and
he returned profoundly agitated by what he witnessed. In an
article he wrote entitled "The America I have Seen," he
conveyed his shock at the degree of materialism, individualism,
racism, and loose sexual mores that he observed both within and
outside the academic community. He also conveyed his repulsion
for the lack of aesthetic tastes he observed in the culture, as well
as for its support of the new state of Israel.

Even before his travel to the United States, Qutb already felt
threatened by the encroachment of American values. On the
boat over he wrote:

> Should I travel to America, and become flimsy and ordinary,
> like those who are satisfied with idle talk and sleep. Or should
> I distinguish myself with values and spirit. Is there other than
> Islam that I should be steadfast to in its character and hold on
> to its instructions, in this life amidst deviant chaos, and the
> endless means of satisfying animalistic desires, pleasures, and
> awful sins? (http://en.wikipedia.org/wiki/Sayyid_Qutb).

Finally, following his two-year stint, he decried the "shocking" people of America, who were "numb to faith in religion, faith in art, and faith in spiritual values altogether" (http://en.wikipedia.org/wiki/Sayyid_Qutb).

Upon his return to Egypt, Qutb's rejection of Western values and Islamic radicalization continued to grow. In the early 1950s he resigned from his civil service job and joined the activist orthodox organization known as the Muslim Brotherhood. Following Nasser's rise to power and subsequent embrace of secular nationalist ideology, Qutb became an increasingly outspoken and visible enemy of the Nasser regime. By the late 1950s, Qutb was imprisoned by Nasser, and gained an increasingly loyal following. Among the followers was a pious 14-year-old boy named Ayman al-Zawahiri. Not only did al-Zawahiri become a student of Qutb's, but he went on to become a close associate of Osama Bin-Laden, and eventually, the "mastermind" of the most notorious terrorist organization in the contemporary world—Al Qaeda.

Both Osama Bin-Laden and Ayman al-Zawahiri represented an intensifying movement of revulsion toward Western—in particular U.S. and Israeli—incursions into the Arab world. Their vitriol was summarized in a 1998 religious ruling or "fatwa" that associates not only with the 1991 U.S. invasion of Iraq in the Gulf War but with the prospective September 11, 2001 terrorist attacks on New York and Washington. A few passages from this acidic yet revealing manifesto will convey its main thrust:

> ...For over seven years the United States has been occupying the lands of Islam in the holiest of places, the Arabian Peninsula, plundering its riches, dictating to its rulers, humiliating its people, terrorizing its neighbors, and turning its bases in the Peninsula into a spearhead through which to fight the neighboring Muslim people.
>
> If some people have in the past argued about the fact of the occupation, all the people of the Peninsula have now acknowledged it. The best proof of this is the Americans' continuing aggression against the Iraqi people using the Peninsula as a staging post....

So here they come to annihilate what is left of this people and to humiliate their Muslim neighbors.

Third, if the Americans' aims behind these wars are religious and economic, the aim is also to serve the Jews' petty state and divert attention from its occupation of Jerusalem and murder of Muslims there. The best proof of this is their eagerness to destroy Iraq, the strongest neighboring Arab state, and their endeavor to fragment all the states of the region such as Iraq, Saudi Arabia, Egypt, and Sudan into paper statelets and through their disunion and weakness to guarantee Israel's survival and the continuation of the brutal crusade occupation of the Peninsula.

All these crimes and sins committed by the Americans are a clear declaration of war on Allah, his messengers, and Muslims...(Federation of American Scientists trans., 23 Feb., 1998, p. 2)

The historical resentment of Western imposition on Arab lands reached a peak following Bush's invasion of Iraq in 2003. The rhetoric of his administration and world view was plain: there is an "axis of evil" that includes the rogue state of Iraq, Saddam Hussein (the dictator of Iraq) "tried to kill [Bush's father]," and other nations are "either with us or against us" in this battle to destroy evil (van Wormer, 2002, p. 4). Bush and his neo-conservative administration also believed that eventually they could reshape the entire Middle East into America's image. "My job isn't to try nuance," Bush concluded in one of his speeches. "I think moral clarity is important. This is evil versus good" (p. 3).

Given this battleground of "black–white" absolutist positioning, it is instructive once again to examine its formation. As with earlier denials of mystery through history, the recent U.S.–Islamic clash centers on a startling leader–follower convergence. In America, a gradual backlash was building against 1960's liberalization and diversification of values (themselves a backlash against the previous era of conservatism). Conservatives, who perceived the sexual, drug-oriented, and dovish dispositions of '60s activists as a threat to their own sense of propriety, became increasingly agitated as a result. The so-called "moral majority" of the early 1970s and the increasingly religious, nationalistic, and materialistic emphases of the 1980s and 1990s emerged as chief outgrowths of these disaffected conservatives (Schlesinger, 1986, pp. 36–37). The failure of the U.S. to "win" the Viet Nam war, and the 2001 attack on the twin towers of the World Trade Center seemed to be perceived as such direct threats to national pride that when Bush declared the preemptive war on Iraq, nearly 80% of the U.S. electorate supported him (Milbank & VandeHei, 2003). For many, a kind of hyper masculinized ideal began to predominate. This ideal lauded the brash and direct just as it spurned the reflective and diplomatic. Nationalism and mercantilism were "in," while dialogue and introspection were "out." By 2005, however, it all began to sour. With news of mounting military as well as civilian deaths, military interrogation scandals, and the virtual collapse of the U.S. economy, the electorate began again to reverse course.

Yet the synchrony between populace and leader during the Bush years could not have been more stark. At the same time that many U.S. citizens felt bereft and deprived of their value, the 43rd president of the United States, George W. Bush, appeared to mirror their travails. While the details of Bush's background are arguable, some facts strike clear: He was the eldest son of a wealthy ex-U.S. president, the brother of a beloved governor, and the heir to a long line of political and military aristocrats (McAdams, 2010). He was also, from much that we can gather, a self-devaluing child, a poor scholar, a dilettante, a drinker, and a failed businessman (Weisberg, 2008). These and related qualities, according to Dan McAdams's psychobiography of Bush, led to a "perfect storm" of personal factors implicated in Bush's decision to launch the Iraq war. McAdams formally identified these factors as follows:

> strong dispositional traits in his personality that can be traced all the way back to his childhood years…a set of motivational goals passed down from one generation to the next in the Bush family, including the desire to defeat his beloved father's greatest enemies…and a personal story of redemption that George W. Bush developed and internalized

for his own life at midlife, and then projected onto the world after the terrorist attacks of 9/11. (McAdams, 2010, p. 8)

McAdams goes on to define this story of redemption in terms that are relevant to many people who felt caught up in and yet ashamed of their role in the libertine ethos of the 1960s, particularly if they mishandled that role or held rigid or conservative ideals. In short, McAdams elaborates, Bush harbored a "personal narrative about moving from sin to salvation, and about recovery through self-discipline..." (p. 9). If this personal narrative sounds familiar in the context of Islamic radicalism—as well as many other radicalisms that we've discussed—that is also no accident. As the astute Hoffer (1951) has pointed out, "a rising mass movement attracts and holds a following not by its doctrine and promises but the refuge it offers from the anxieties, barrenness, and meaninglessness of individual existence" (p. 44). He goes on:

"Though they seem at opposite poles, fanatics of all kinds are actually crowded together at one end. It is the fanatic and the moderate who are poles apart and never meet....it is easier for a fanatic Communist [for example,] to be converted to fascism, chauvinism, or Catholicism than to become a sober liberal" (p. 81)

The Challenge to the World
Today the sense of insignificance (and its resultant denial) is roiling the developing world. It can be felt from Wall Street to Islamabad and from Beijing to Mexico City. At the crux of this problem is still the frantic drive for *certainty*, but this drive is taking on new and diversifying forms, spurring wider personal and social divisions.

The chain of consequences issuing from this crisis is alarming. The fanatical drive for financial certainty, for example, fueled the virtual collapse of the world banking system in 2008. It enabled the spillage of millions of gallons of crude oil in the Gulf of New Mexico in 2009; and it fostered a near melt down of the Fukushima nuclear facility in northern Japan in 2011. What are the future disasters-in-waiting?

To compound this situation, the frenzy for profits is fueling the pharmaceutical industry, which now pushes an array of questionable drugs on unwary consumers. As of this writing (2012), approximately 10 percent of Americans over six are on a medication for depression, and over the last four decades, drugs have become the "dominant mode of treatment" for both children and adults (Angell, 2011, p. 20). Such desperation for remedies seems at least partly attributable to the cultural conditions outlined above. If corporations saturate the media with simplistic products, then consumers will foster simplistic lifestyles—and these lifestyles have consequences. Sometimes these consequences are benign, such as strained eyes from the overuse of television, but too often the consequences are injurious or even lethal. The latter are illustrated not only by the schemers and plotters of Wall Street, but by the addicts and militants on Main Street. They are evident in the push-button indifference of war strategists, the superhero machismo of gang leaders, and even the power-seeking grandiosities of serial killers.

While simplistic or hollow lifestyles are fostered by the frenzy for profits, they are also fueled by the drive for religious or ideological salvation. The more that people fear life's complexity the more they tend toward ready forms of resolution. Yet as Eric Hoffer (1951) has observed, and events of the past 5000 years have demonstrated, resolutions too often become fixations and fixations fanaticisms. Consider, for example, two contemporary yet widely divergent voices from the political right and left: The following statement is from the "Tea Party" conservative and 2012 presidential candidate Michelle Bachmann on homosexuality. While acknowledging that her own sister is gay, and warning that gay marriage would lead to schoolchildren being indoctrinated into a gay lifestyle, she stated: "This is not funny. It's a very sad life. It's part of Satan, I think, to say that this [lifestyle] is gay" (Goldberg, 2011, June 14). Bachmann's husband Marcus, who "treats" gay people in his counseling practice was even more emphatic: "Barbarians need to be educated. They need to be disciplined, and just because someone feels this or thinks this, doesn't mean that we're supposed to go down that road" (Goldberg, 2011).

Now juxtapose the latter to the dumbfounding words of the leftist French philosopher Michel Foucault, who ironically was heroically gay but also rabidly anti-Western. Sounding more like a revolutionary from the Terror than a French scholar, Foucault raged at Western (and no doubt heterosexual) chauvinism in an explosive 1971 tirade against the "ruling class":

> The proletariat [working class] doesn't wage war against the ruling class because it considers such a war to be just. The proletariat makes war against the ruling class because, for the first time in history, it wants to take power. When the proletariat takes power, it may be quite possible that the proletariat will exert toward the classes over which it has triumphed a violent, dictatorial, even bloody power. I can't see what objection could possibly be made of this. (Lila, 2001, p. 150)

Within a span of ten years, Foucault, the theorist of personal empowerment and freedom, not only aligned himself with the French Maoist movement known as "The Maoist Gauche Proletarienne," but became a supporter of the 1979 Iranian revolution.   According to Lila (2001), he reveled "in the 'intoxication' of revolution and the violent expression of 'collective will,' and praised its leaders' 'political spirituality,' which he thought reflected a healthy 'religion of combat and sacrifice'" (p. 154).   Within five years, and following a period of defiant promiscuity, Foucault succumbed to AIDS (Lila, 2001).

The problem with polarization, then, is not only that it rigidifies a given group or individual, but that it contaminates the groups or individuals that are touched by it.   To the extent that polarization sets itself *against* others, it sets others against it; and to the degree it accomplishes that, it sets people up to destroy. On the other hand, polarization is not *all* knee-jerk and destructive; it can have redemptive elements—such as the aspiration for justice, or a vision of stability.   The problem, however, is that the panic that underlies so much of the polarized mentality, distorts the redemptive elements into destructive extremes.   Hence, Bachman was so concerned about the rapid changes in sexual mores in society (as well as in her family) that she became fanatical herself to oppose those changes.

Correspondingly, Foucault was so incensed by the oppression he experienced from those associated with the political right that he pleaded, in turn, for the oppression of those associated with the political right. And the cycle goes on.

Today, the problem with polarization is many-sided. Bachman's estrangement from her gay sister and Foucault's victimization at the hands of his patriarchal oppressors are but singular examples of a much wider phenomenon that comprises increasing divisions among increasingly polarized groups. These groups live relatively harmoniously within their own communities but experience almost complete isolation from other groups that also exhibit such cohesion.

In "The Big Sort," Bill Bishop (2008) makes the trenchant point that these encapsulated groups are permeating America, and that they may soon envelop the world. Paradoxically, while social networks are binding disparate geographies and cultures, they are, at the same time, homogenizing the regions they bind. If a person is polarized toward left wing liberalism, for example, it is increasingly easy for that person to surround herself or himself with left wing (and self-reinforcing) social networks, news, and entertainment. The same is true, correspondingly, for the right wing conservative, or the academic, or person of color, and so on. Due in part to our technology and in part to the ease of polarized living, we seem to be nearing a matrix of encapsulation, where rich are severed from poor, urbanites are walled off from agrarians, educated are divided from uneducated, and religious are split from secular. Here is what Bishop (2008) reported about America's last 30 years:

- People with college degrees were relatively evenly spread across the nation's cities in 1970. Thirty years later, college graduates had congregated in particular cities, a phenomenon that decimated the economies in some places and caused other regions to flourish.

- The generation of ministers who built sprawling mega-churches in the new suburbs learned to attract stadium-sized congregations through the "homogenous unit principle." The new churches were designed for cookie-cutter parishioners, what one church-growth proponent described as "people like us."

• In 1976 only about a quarter of America's voters lived in a county a presidential candidate won by a landslide margin. By 2004, it was nearly half.

• Businesses learned to target their marketing to like-minded "image-tribes," a technique used by Republicans in the 2004 campaign.

Bishop concludes:

Living in politically like-minded groups has had its consequences. People living in homogenous communities grow both more extreme and more certain in their beliefs. Locally, therefore, governments backed by large majorities are tackling every conceivable issue. Nationally, however, Congress has lost most of its moderate members. (http://www.thebigsort.com/book.php)

What seems evident here is that those with the technical means can now plug into an astounding variety of emotionally and culturally sanctioned denial systems. With the stroke of a key, wounds can be bypassed and mysteries breezily dismissed. All people need to do is to press a few buttons, stick closely to their virtual communities, and shirk life's complexities. They can text one another, but to what extent can they really speak to one another? They can watch one another on screens, but to what extent can they risk crossing over into one anothers' worlds, exploring together, discovering together, and learning how to get along together?

Ironically, such crossing over is probably happening as much or more than ever in certain quarters (such as in thriving multicultural communities or in therapeutic groups). But by and large people seem to be separating from and opposing one another; and at the extremes of this movement seems to be the same time-tested blight that fed the fanaticism of Greek and Roman tyrants; fueled the zealotry of Pope Urban, Stalin, and Hitler; and left its mark in the sands and jungles and streets of every major sector of the world. It is the blight of insignificance, which breeds desperation. And when this desperation is not addressed it leads to polarization, distortion, and, ultimately, the quick-fix model for living.

Today, more than ever perhaps, we are besieged by the quick-fix model for living. Some of these quick fixes are conveniences; they make our lives more comfortable, healthful, and productive. But some also suck the life out of us, particularly when they are manipulated by entrenched commercial or ideological interests. Such interests foster enormously seductive distortions, privilege one product or idea over all others, and prey on unfounded fears (just consider all the ideas and products that were created in the name of social status, unlimited opportunity, physical or sexual power, and carefree living). Wars have been launched over these illusions, reckless or indulgent lifestyles, and robotic adherence to rules. In November, 2012, in fact, the U.S. Congress was on the brink of freezing its debt ceiling and defaulting on its credit because of such illusions. The seduction of unregulated free markets (unlimited opportunity), on the one hand, and bloated (carefree) bureaucracy, on the other, has all but vanquished flexible and pragmatic alternatives.

Thus, the quick-fix model for living appears to be the chief polarization today, underlying all other polarizations of consequence. It runs through our political organizations, our educational system, our work life, our dietary habits, our psychological and medical treatments, our religious and consumer preferences, and even our social networks. While there are undeniably hopeful signs amid this quick-fix mania— including the expansion of personal choices, the acceleration of learning, and the diversification of knowledge—it remains to be seen whether these hopeful signs will lead to more vivacious and discerning lives. If history is any clue, then the outlook is bleak. Yet if there is anything that this book is intended to show, it is that history can (and must!) be learned from, and the major learning I have gleaned is that the number one blight in the world is polarization. It murders souls as well as bodies, and the sooner we address it, the sooner we grant humanity a chance.

In the next, and final, section of the book, we will turn to the monumental task of how to address polarized, mystery-denying minds. We will do this first by examining an alternative to polarization: awe-based psychology predicated on psychological depth research. Then we will search out how this alternative has been lived out through history (including in parts of the same mystery-denying cultures we have just considered). Finally, we will look at how the alternative might be lived out in the face of present-day realities.

PART 2

WHAT WE CAN DO ABOUT THE POLARIZED MIND

It is not that man is 'evil,' but he is not 'neutral' either. He is terribly afraid of his own death, and of the insignificance of his life, his 'creatureliness.' And so, his whole life is a protest that he 'is somebody,' and this protest he takes out on others: he will even kill them to show that he can triumph over death. I think that the theoretical problem for our time is to harmonize this knowledge with the possibility of a humanistic science...

--*Ernest Becker in a letter to Professor Momin (undated)*
(From the Ernest Becker Papers, Columbia University)

This is the whole point that most people miss. The natural IS the supernatural! Creation IS the primary miracle. 'Sin' means the failure to appreciate the miracle of creation—period; the secularization of it, the cutting up of it into realms of categories. This is what Tillich meant by urging that we get back to a 'belief-ful' realism; belief that the real world is a miracle.

--*Ernest Becker, in a Letter to Professor David Fee, 1968*
(From the Ernest Becker Papers, Columbia University)

Chapter 4

The Embrace Of Mystery Through History: Awe, Wisdom, and the Fluid Center of Life

In the first section of this book we considered how mystery denial and polarization have decimated lives. In this section we look at the radiant exceptions to the latter—the ways in which mystery has been acknowledged, grappled with, and embraced, in many cases by the same power centers we have critiqued. It is my contention that by studying people who have not only rejected but also *affirmed* their enigmatic roots, we can obtain a foothold on reform.

Toward an Awe-Based Reformation

Awe is our fundamental relationship to mystery; and mystery is the essence of being. Although awe has been defined in myriad ways throughout history, I have understood it as our humility and wonder—or sense of adventure—toward living (Schneider, 2004, 2009).[6]

The distinguishing feature of awe is paradox. It is the realization that we are both moldering dust and glittering gods, and that our solace lies between those extremes. This is a formidable problem, to be sure. Yet, in my view, it is imperative to address this problem if we are to survive. While the polarized mind seeks refuge in one side or the other of this paradoxical condition, either inflating our god-likeness (as in a Caesar or

---

[6] In the parlance of experimental psychology awe is the experience of vastness (e.g., a panoramic view, the birth of a child, a great work of art) that cannot be fully assimilated and, as a result, evokes wonder and an alteration of consciousness (see Keltner & Haidt, 2003). The unifying theme here is that awe pertains to both our apartness from, as well as participation in, the daunting nature of existence.

Napoleon) or accentuating our worm-likeness (as in the equation of native Americans with "savages"), the awe-based mind reaches for a very different assessment of its own and others' lives. For example, whereas the polarized mind seeks comfort in one-sided "solutions," the "awe-based" mind seeks growth in many-sided engagements. And whereas the polarized mind thrives on panic-driven reaction, the awe-based mind thrives on present-centered response.

Put another way, the awe-based mind is both fluid (adventurous) and yet centered (discerning); it courts neither compulsive expansion nor rigid constriction but a fullness of choice and dexterity of response.

Awe as the Scaffolding for Wisdom, Wisdom as the Guidance System for Awe

Most of the constructive contributions through history have exhibited the qualities of a fluidly centered, awe-based mind. Mass movements that have endured, like aspects of the American Revolution, have been both humble and bold (consider George Washington declining to become a monarch, or John Adams refusing mob justice). Religious leaders—such as Martin Luther King, Mahatma Gandhi, Guatama Buddha, and Jesus—all responded boldly in the face of oppression but, equally, they all responded humbly, compassionately, and discerningly before the fragilities of life. These lessons are not lost on people of all walks of life (consider also Nelson Mandela, Mother Teresa, Tich Naht Han, and Rumi). It is not by accident that cultures the world over admire many qualities of the awe-based mind. Just consider the degree and frequency to which "awe" is invoked by world religions, philosophies, and artistic traditions (e.g., see Bonner & Friedman, 2011 for a review).

That which psychologists call "wisdom" can also be understood as a product of the awe-based mind. In his comprehensive review, Stephen Hall (2010), surveyed all the major wisdom philosophies throughout the ages and concluded that they comprised eight "pillars" of psycho-neural functioning: emotional regulation, prioritization, moral acuity, compassion, humility, altruism, patience, and coping with uncertainty. Dilip Jeste, president of the American Psychiatric Association in 2012, also studied wisdom across history and cultures and found virtually the same time-honored qualities. Among these were:

a pragmatic experience-based knowledge of life, reflective and self-reflective capacities, effective dealings with uncertainty and ambiguity, [a]...tolerance for the varying views/perceptions of others, emotional stability, prosocial attitudes, [a] recognition of the need for multiple perspectives, [an awareness of] the limits of knowledge, and [an openness to] compromise. (cited in Walsh, 2011, p. 11)

Finally, Robert Sternberg in his extensive synthesis found that wisdom can be distilled into the following formulation: "the application of intelligence, creativity, and knowledge as mediated by values toward the achievement of a common good through a *balance* among (a) intrapersonal (b) interpersonal, (c) extrapersonal interests..." (Sternberg, Reznitskaya, & Jarvin, 2007, p. 145). In essence, Hall, Jeste, and Sternberg characterize wisdom as *both* humbling (e.g., discerning, deliberating, compassionate) *and* emboldening (e.g., wondering, venturing, discovering). They view flexibility and the capacity to (affectively, cognitively, and intuitively) *respond to,* as opposed to merely *react against* people or problems, as key to wise functioning.

Abraham Maslow (1968) has also elaborated on an awe-based wisdom paradigm with his study of self-actualizing individuals. In these investigations, he identified a range of traits that distinguished self-actualizers as a cohesive group. For example, he noted that his subjects "attained a 'second naiveté'...Their innocence of perception and expressiveness was combined with sophisticated minds" (p. 138). He also noted that self-actualizing people were "relatively unfrightened by the unknown, the mysterious," and the "puzzling." And they were "often positively attracted by" those dimensions, selecting them "to meditate on, and to be absorbed with" (p. 138). "They do not neglect the unknown," he elaborated,

or try to make believe it is really known, nor do they organize, dichotomize, or rubricize it prematurely. They do not cling to the familiar, nor is their quest for the truth a catastrophic need for certainty, safety, definiteness, and order....They can be, when the total objective situation calls for it, comfortably disorderly, sloppy-anarchic, chaotic, vague, doubtful, uncertain, indefinite, approximate, inexact, or inaccurate (all at certain moments in science, art, or life in general, quite desirable). (p. 139)

On the other hand, Maslow did not downplay the capacity of his self-actualizing subjects to be firm and incisive alongside their radical openness. "One observation I made has puzzled me for many years," Maslow wrote, but has begun "to fall into place now. It was what I described as the resolution of dichotomies in self-actualizing people. Briefly stated, I found that I had to see differently many oppositions and polarities that all psychologists had taken for granted as straight line continua" (p. 139). For instance, he concluded:

These most mature of all people were also strongly childlike. These same people, the strongest egos ever described and the most definitely individual, were also precisely the ones who could be most easily ego-less, self-transcending and problem centered. (p. 140)

Now compare these above descriptions with those by people who claimed to have been transformed by the sense of awe and notice how compatible they are. Bonner and Friedman (2011) for example, found that six people who claimed to have been transformed by a sense of awe homed in on ten essential themes: a sense of *profundity*, a sense of *connectedness*, a sense of the *numinous* (or holy), an awareness of *fear*, an awareness of *vastness, existential awareness* (or the experience of being itself), *openness and acceptance, ineffable wonder, presence,* and *heightened perception.*

Finally, we now have direct experimental evidence linking awe with prosocial, wisdom-based behavior. In a series of studies investigating awe and prosocial attitudes, Stanford researchers Melanie Rudd and her colleagues found that inspiring awe—even more than "happiness"—correlated with an increased patience, an increased desire to help others through voluntary activity, reduced materialism, and an increase in life satisfaction (Rudd, Vohs, & Aaker, 2012). In another study, experimentally induced awe associated with increased desire to visit spiritual as distinct from hedonistic travel destinations (e.g., Tibet vs. prequake Haiti) and increased feelings of oneness with others in general and friends in particular (Van Cappellen & Saroglou, 2012).

While some may quibble with the definitions, it is evident that both wisdom and self-actualization begin with awe. They are both built, for example, on profound humility, awareness of vulnerability, and acceptance of destiny, but they are equally rooted in appreciative wonder, tenacious courage, and elevated vision. They both acknowledge the foundational mystery of being, but they also, and equally encounter that fundamental mystery. This dialectical approach of acknowledgement and encounter is critical, for if you can't *acknowledge* the mystery then you end up being polarized, i.e., imperious, petty, narrow, and intolerant. If you can't *encounter* the mystery then you end up being inert, i.e., helpless, stuck, depleted, and ineffectual.

The attainment of what may be called character, therefore, is dependent on both acknowledgement of and encounter with the mystery of being (Mendelowitz, 2008). This is what enables the wise to self-regulate, prioritize, make meaningful moral judgments, and exhibit compassion, humility, and tolerance. It is what enables self-actualizers to experience wholeness, perfection, justice, aliveness, richness, simplicity, beauty, goodness, uniqueness, effortlessness, playfulness, truth, and self-sufficiency. The question is how do the wise and self-actualizing develop their awe-based traits? If awe is a birthright, and there is good reason to believe that it is (e.g., see Pearsall, 2007); if it is that commingling of dread, veneration, and wonder so characteristic of youth, then how can it be shaped so that it does not disintegrate as we age so that it can be set free, deepened, and refined? How does one develop the balance or centering ability to bring awe into the day-to-day tumult of contemporary life? To answer these questions we need to turn first to how awe is cultivated—nourished, refined, channeled—in childhood, then to its path through adulthood, and finally to its impact on the world.

Instilling Wisdom at the Root: Childrearing

The best parents, in my view, combine expansive vision with contractive focus.   They are authoritative—more than and in contrast to either being permissive or authoritarian (Baumrind, 1971). By authoritative, I mean a parenting style that appreciates the paradoxes of human life, awe, and the ever-present capacity to evolve. I mean a style that embraces spontaneous play just as it does disciplined work, and that is acutely attuned to the timeliness—that is, appropriateness—for living engagement. This may sound classically like Sternberg's notion of balance, but it is not simply static balance or the Greek notion of moderation; it is dynamic balance—balance in the face of continual change and need for adjustment.   Like life itself, parenting is an exercise in versatile management, where neither isolated fluidity nor containment will suffice.

If we want to cultivate a society of wise adults, therefore, we need to instill some abilities that may not seem all that wise at first. We need to take some risks that may not make us or our children feel comfortable. We need to expand our ideas about comfort, as well as challenge and discipline, if we are to ignite the awe-based fires.

For example, how many parents (in Western societies at least) expose their children to the *inexplicable* with as much urgency as they expose them to the explicable and known? How many parents purposely raise questions with their charges, introduce them to puzzling myths or stories, and support them to experience the power of those encounters? How many take them on physical or intellectual adventures or point to adventures as they arise (such as the exhilaration of thunder or the arrangement of stars).   While children are quite naturally exposed to the inexplicable (e.g., through their play, their curiosity about nature etc.), all too rarely it seems are they taught to prize that inexplicability, to immerse themselves in it, and to see where it leads.

There is of, course, a very wide gradient with respect to exposure of children to the inexplicable, and many different ranges of tolerance among individuals, cultures, and civilizations. But one point seems evident. The examples of awe-based, authoritative childrearing are scant, and what we are left with (even across cultures) tends either to be conformist (ritualized) or polarizing (authoritarian). If this weren't the case, we would not see all the destruction that has been wrought in the name of "traditional" parenting. We would not see the sense of insignificance—as manifested in rates of depression, boredom, drug taking, religious and ideological fanaticism, and criminality—as such a world-crushing problem. In short, we would see a different world.

While it would be the height of hubris to presume the details of this world, we do have hints.

We have hints in the lives of activists and visionaries who at various points benefited from authoritative, awe-based caretaking, whether that caretaking took the form of an inspiring parent, an inspiring friend, or an inspiring idea. Dean Keith Simonton (1994), for example, found that the parents of eminent artists and scientists tended to encourage a great "love of learning" in their homes, enriching their children's development with conversations, books, and hobbies that "stimulate[d] them intellectually, aesthetically, and culturally" (pp. 157–158). Interestingly, Simonton also found that life difficulties stimulated greatness. He cited a study in which fully 53% of 699 eminent figures in world history had lost a parent (often the father) by age 26 (p. 153). He also cited studies of the rampant alcoholism, marital difficulties, and abuses that took place in some of these households—and the picture that emerges here is that tragedy often accompanies life growth. The question, however, is how do the caretakers handle these difficulties? What separates the caregivers of those who emerge and indeed thrive in the face of such backgrounds from those who merely function, or worse, decompensate into abusers?

We are provided critical insight into these questions in a work by Alice Miller (1990) called *The Untouched Key*. In this book, Miller found that although some of the world's greatest criminals (such as Hitler and Stalin) shared similar calamitous backgrounds with eminent visionaries (such as Picasso and Nietzsche), one difference stood out; whereas Hitler and Stalin received virtually no relief from their traumatic environments, visionaries such as Nietzsche and Picasso encountered what Miller termed "helpful witnesses" to soothe their difficulties.

Miller wrote of Picasso, for example, that if it wasn't for his father's "sheltering arms," his whole "terrifying experience" of almost having been stillborn and crushed by the Malaga earthquake at three years old might have crippled him. But "thanks to [his father's] protective care," she elaborated, Picasso "was able to store what he saw in a way that permitted him to keep expressing it in new forms in his art" (p. 16). There must be "helping witnesses," Miller summarized, for optimal development to take root (p. 148). "Above all," she concluded, there must be caretakers, including "nannies, house-hold staff, aunts, uncles, siblings, or grandparents...who [are] not camouflaging cruelty as love because they had experienced love in their own childhoods" (p. 148).

From a similar standpoint, Gina O'Connel Higgens (1994) conducted a study of a cohort she termed "resilient adults." These adults suffered brutal childhoods at the hands of remarkably dysfunctional parents. On the other hand, these adults also encountered—for varying periods—helping witnesses (or "surrogates," as O'Connel Higgens called them) who epitomized awe-based caretakers. O'Connel Higgens identified three major characteristics of such effective surrogacy: (1) A relationship that energizes the "receiver as well as the giver...to create something that is deeply life-sustaining to the resilient overcomer" (p. 114), (2) the communication from surrogates that overcomers "were deeply special and important simply by being who they were" (p. 114), and (3) the encouragement from surrogates for overcomers to "let their talents unfold, whatever those strengths might be" (p. 115).

The great challenge, of course—and the challenge we have undertaken in this volume—is how to model a society based on authoritative and awe-based witnessing. Are there any models that currently exist? Have they existed historically in part or in whole. We now will plumb these challenging issues, beginning with the power centers we have already considered.

When History Embraces Mystery:
Power Centers Reconsidered

As we have seen, the encounter with mystery can terrorize, and it can also bring about terrifying results. At first this terror may pertain to a particular event, such as an earthquake, or an object, such as a beast of prey; but at a deeper level it appears to encompass our entire condition, our entire sense of helplessness before existence. One can find traces of these reactions in the earliest known drawings on caves. They depict menacing bison and growling tigers. Paleolithic tribes, according to Rudolf Otto (1923), stood similarly before the puzzlements of nature. The chaos of storms, the crackle of thunder, and the bewilderment of the night rattled the hardiest huntsman. But terror is only one side of the equation. Eventually, and with the mustering of courage, early peoples also found a contrasting element in their responses—fascination.

At the same time that tribes quaivered before the upheavals of nature, they also began to wonder about it, depict it in legends, and study its forms. At the same time that some were struck with paralysis, others were stirred to pay homage, inquire, and explore. These attitudes formed the basis for the oldest known myths and legends of humanity.

Sumerian Wisdom
In the earliest known Sumerian text, the Enuma Elish, we have seen how the forces of chaos (existence) had to be tamed by the forces of order (the male sea god Aspu and the female sea god Tiamat). We have also seen how their children, led by Ea, began to rebel against this order, and eventually to overtake it. These children also developed new and more powerful gods to perform their handiwork—Marduk being the exemplar. However, there is another side to this early Sumerian parable. The story not only depicts the desperation to control the chaos with ever more powerful gods (leaders); it also illuminates the relative coexistence with chaos and the perils in attendance for those who reject that coexistence. This point is illustrated initially by the comparatively peaceful world of the original parents, Aspu and Tiamat. Both born of the sea, Aspu and Tiamat embodied natural connections to the vast unknown, to the evolving, and to existence itself. They also seemed to get along with their environment, at least initially, and spawned productive communities, families, and land.

Hence, the story implies, there is something valuable about living naturally, moderately, and with prudence. The advent of rebellious children, however, changed this whole scenario. Not only were the children insolent, they were demanding and irreverent. They seemed not to care at all about what preceded them, and sought mainly to gratify their vanity.

On the other hand, it also seems clear that Aspu and Tiamat had trouble with change, the natural evolution of succeeding generations, and the idea that their hard work could be savaged. In this light, Aspu—not unlike many patriarchs through subsequent history—not only attempted to discipline his children but to annihilate them (at least in the case of Ea). I believe the implication here is that even prudent caretakers can turn fanatical, and that existential helplessness is a companion of all. The challenge is to work with that helplessness, recognize its naturalness, and develop capacities to respond to rather than react against its ferocity. Hence, one way that Aspu could have responded was to talk to his children, support them in their separateness but also remind them of their impudence and all that could be lost by their short-sightedness.

The epic of *Gilgamesh*, some years later, also illustrates the folly of reactionary and, therefore, polarized action. But this was only side of the story. Recall, first, the polarized version: Gilgamesh, accompanied by his friend, Enkidu, set out to rescue their home village by bringing cedar wood back from a haunted forest. While they succeed in their quest, they also become arrogant in the process. They kill Humbaba, the guardian of the cedar wood, despite knowingly upsetting Humbaba's protector, Enhill. Upon Gilgamesh's return to his people, he summarily rejects the advances of a female goddess, and Enkidu loses his humility. Enkidu is then killed for his transgression, and Gilgamesh, partly in mourning for his friend, goes off in search of everlasting life. But Gilgamesh's mission also is cut short, for, as a higher god explained, "You were given kingship," Gilgamesh. "Such was your destiny; everlasting life was not your destiny" (Sandars, 1972, p. 118).

But *Gilgamesh* was a story of maturation as much if not more than a tale of immaturity. As the poet who relates the story tells us, the story of Gilgamesh is a profound reflection on youth and age, triumph and despair, men and gods, and life and death. "Read out," he declares in his prologue to the story, "the travails of Gilgamesh, [and] all that he went through" (George, 1999, p. xxxv). What Gilgamesh "went through" was a series of "wake-up calls" about what it means to encounter life in its complexity, its depths, and its constraints. He learns that he is indeed capable of great things, that he can achieve more than he ever conceived. But he also learns that it all comes with a price, and that the ultimate price—death—cannot be dodged.

Gilgamesh, the authorities inform us, is the philosophical template for many classic wisdom teachings to come, particularly in the Near East. The biblical passage known as the *Proverbs*, for example is closely related, as is the ancient Egyptian text "Instructions of Amen-em-Opet," as well as Greek and Roman mythologies about heroic adventurers.

The Light of Judaism
While the Hebrew Bible, as noted earlier, is replete with stories of arrogant transgression, it is also rich with instruction about living an awe-based life. The injunction against idol worship, for example, can be understood as an encouragement to reach for the furthest "beyond" as Ernest Becker (1973) put it, unconstrained by provincial or pedantic deities. It can also be interpreted as supporting inquiry, imagination, and creativity, as well as human responsibility; for if the rain god or god of the harvest cannot be readily called upon, then there is a greater role for the ingenuity of the farmer, and so on.

Of course the monotheistic God (Yahweh) can also be provincial and pedantic, as we have seen. Yahweh is brash with His show of power, and wields it at will. He is absolute about certain moral precepts, such as fidelity to His commandments, and he smites those who threaten that authority. At the same time, however, there is a liberating elusiveness about Yahweh that challenges people to achieve a new level of faith. In the story of Job, for example, Yahweh's motives are almost completely hidden. Job is tormented by Him but he has no idea why. He is a good and pious man—the usual qualifications for divine reward—and yet he's crushed at every turn.

"If my anguish were weighed," Job cries, "it would be heavier than the sand of the sea....God's terrors are arrayed against me" (Tanakh, Job, 6.4).

But several lines later, after much inner searching, Job begins to recognize an opportunity in his calamity. He begins to see that the acknowledgment of mystery is the beginning of wisdom, and that it is the complacent who suffer above all. He declares: "In the thought of the complacent there is contempt for calamity; [yet] it is ready for those whose foot slips. Robbers live untroubled in their tents. And those who provoke God are secure" (Job, 12.5).

For Job, then, as with Jewish prophesy, it is not the honestly searching individual that ultimately loses out but the one who spurns mystery, and as a consequence, life's depth.

The Greek Awakening
The Greek "awe-wakening" spanned roughly 1500 to 500 B.C.E. By the fifth century, the Greek city-state of Athens became a Mecca of wisdom about mystery. Between the philosopher Socrates, and playwrights Aeschylus, Sophocles, and Euripides, a budding worldview took shape. This worldview was modeled around three life challenges: necessity—or individual destiny; fate—or divine rule beyond the individual; and heroic virtue—or the struggle of the individual to master his/her destiny in the face of society and fate (Ambrosio, 2009). One of the paradigmatic examples of this worldview was the athletic contest. Sport enabled individuals to grapple with their destiny (e.g., talent for running), face their fate (e.g., triumph or loss), and serve their community (e.g., by their example).

Another equally important example of the Greek worldview was the model of the citizen-hero, as embodied by Socrates (Ambrosio, 2009). For Socrates, the "highest wisdom is to know that you do not know" (p. 18). Or as Plato recorded it in *The Apology*, Socrates' trial for the "corruption" of Athenian youth, Socrates states: "The fact is that [none] of us knows anything beautiful and good," though many people "think they know." "So", he concludes, "I am wiser than [they] by only this trifle, that what I do not know I don't think I do" (Plato, 1984, p. 427).

It is through the wisdom of uncertainty then that Socrates proceeds. The fresh model he provides to the world addresses necessity, fate, and heroic virtue—but through the "contest" of dialogue rather than sport. In Socrates' form of dialogue, people are challenged to look within themselves, to reappraise their values, and to clarify those values that are most meaningful to them.

There are no certain outcomes in Socrates' world, but there are vital choices. Some of those choices, such as those fueled by arrogance, tend toward calamity, whereas others, such as those fostered by discernment, tend toward personal and interpersonal betterment. Examples of Socrates' wisdom permeate Greek literature and myth. In Herodotus's history of Greek wars, for example, the combatant who displays overreaching pride (or hubris) is often defeated. In Homer's *Odyssey*, struggle is greeted with victory, while presumption is met with calamity. In Sophocles' *Oedipus*, impulsivity is distinguished from wisdom. While Oedipus killed his father through blind rage; the blind "seer" Tiresias helps him to "see" through that blindness to a wider world (May, 1991).

The balancing of self-mastery and fate is summarized by Friedrich Nietzsche in his classic study of Greek literature called *The Birth of Tragedy*. In this opus, Nietzsche identified the essential tension of Greek drama as a clash between two Greek gods—Apollo and Dionysius. Whereas Apollo represented the forces of reason (e.g., self-mastery), Dionysius symbolized the forces of transcendence (e.g., self-abandon). For the Greeks, according to Nietzsche, neither Apollonian reason nor Dionysian transcendence flourished in isolation; healthy living required the balancing of both. As we reflect on the great Greek dramas, we see the penetrating truth of these observations. A dynamic life in these stories arose primarily in connection with *both* self-mastery and self-abandon. The question was, at what point does one grapple with individual achievement and at what point does one give oneself over to the gods? At what point does one discipline and order one's life, and at what point does one abandon these elements for faith or hope in the forces beyond? "Amor fati," Nietzsche once cried, meaning roughly—know when to "love your fate" (Nietzsche, cited in Kaufmann, 1968, p. 416); or as Socrates might have put it, know how to "care for your soul."

Finally, Socrates' worldview can be detected in the institutions of Greek governance and Greek law. Socratic questioning is the basis for social democracy, and social democracy, despite its shortcomings in ancient Greek society, has become recognized as one of the most productive forms of ethical decision making known to humanity. By stressing inquiry, deliberation, and truth—as best as they can be attained—social democracy forms a hedge against all manner of presumption. It upholds reason, but it also protects views that may challenge and prove superior to reason. The issue, as William James (1907/1963) much later elaborated, is not whether a view is absolutely true, but whether it proves helpful to those who are most affected by it. But perhaps the greatest example of Socrates' worldview was summed up at his trial. While reflecting on his exploits, he stated: "The greatest good for a man every day [is] to discuss virtue and the other things about which you hear me talking…[for a] life without enquiry is not worth living…" (Plato, 1984, p. 443).

The Glory of Rome
While ancient Rome was to a large extent an offspring of ancient Greece, it had a radically different focus. Whereas Greece was occupied with the destiny and fate of nature, Rome was fixated on the destiny and fate of Rome (Ambrosio, 2009). This didn't mean that Greece was unconcerned with Greece or that Rome was indifferent to the natural world, but that Rome itself took precedence over much that had been previously established.

The occupation with empire had several major consequences. First, it meant that virtually all devotions, creeds, enrichments, and ambitions were turned toward the glorification of Rome. Second, it meant that those who sought contemplation or inquiry did so at great personal risk. Third, it indicated that individual destiny and cosmic fate intertwined intimately with the state; and fourth, it pointed to a new and emerging technological emphasis—an emphasis that not only adorned infrastructures, such as colossal palaces, but bolstered the most fearsome fighting operation known to the ancient world.

The awesomeness of Rome then was not so much found in the contemplation of individual philosophers but in the philosophies of those who in one way or another contributed to the expansionist requirements of the state. These philosophies included the building of great armies, such as Caesar had achieved, the construction of brilliant temples, and the formation of dazzling villas, arenas, and waterways. The Greek emphasis on self-mastery became channeled into the Roman emphasis, for those who could afford it, on the beautification of the external world. And for those who couldn't afford these luxuries, or who chose a more inward path, the Roman philosophy of Stoicism offered great solace.

Stoicism helped people cope where coping was in short supply, where servitude and hardship reigned. The great philosophers who responded to these agonizing circumstances found in Stoicism a helpful remedy—"learn to live with highly limited options." For example, Epictetus (55 C.E. to 135 C.E.) who was enslaved from birth, wrote:

> Practice then from the start to say to every harsh impression, "You are an impression, and not at all the thing you appear to be." Then examine...whether the impression has to do with the things that are up to us, or those that are not; and if it has to do with the things that are not up to us, be ready to reply, "It is nothing to me." (from chapter 1 of *The Enchiridion*)

In another place he observed:

> Men are disturbed, not by things, but by the principles and notions which they form concerning things. Death, for instance, is not terrible, else it would have appeared so to Socrates. But the terror consists in our notion of death that it is terrible. When therefore we are hindered, or disturbed, or grieved, let us never attribute it to others, but to ourselves; that is, to our own principles. (from chapter 5 of *The Enchiridion*)

In a sense, then, Epictetus was our first cognitive psychologist. He attributed psychological problems not so much to the problems themselves but to the attitudes we take toward them. Instead of merely capitulating to his enslavement, for example, he found ways to relate to it that were empowering to himself. In a sense, this is what we all are challenged to do, particularly if we are in peril. We are challenged not just to alter the peril, which may not work, but to choose attitudes toward that peril that can lift us and help us cope. This was also Viktor Frankl's strategy centuries later when he was able to glimpse the beauty of the Bavarian Alps on the way to a Nazi Death camp. It has further been the strategy of countless others who have managed to live—perhaps even thrive—in spite of their difficulties. In sum, Roman Stoicism is yet another path to awe-based living. By drawing on inner resources, such as one's attitude, one is freed to experience the adventure of life in spite (and in light) of the numerous threats to its sustainment. Ancient Rome was particularly hard for awe-based inquirers, but Epictetus's challenge to creatively respond to, rather than collapse before, entrenched conditions is a call that has resounded through time.

Of Christian Humanism

The single greatest Christian teaching (which was in essence a Jewish teaching) is that no matter who you are or what you have done you are at base accepted. The founder of Christianity, Jesus Christ, elaborated on this teaching in virtually all of his alleged acts. Consider, for example, his treatment of the poor and underprivileged, his willingness to forgive, and his embrace of strangers. It was exemplified in statements such as "Love thy neighbor as thyself" and "Come unto me all ye that labor and are heavy laden, and I will give ye rest" (Smith, 1986, p. 415). It was illustrated by his treatment of a local prostitute, Mary Magdalene, as a *person,* not merely a body. Finally, it was elucidated in his act of martyrdom on behalf of those who followed his path of love.

In this sense, and against entrenched traditions of degradation, Christianity preached humanism. While the practical application of this humanism has wavered wildly throughout history, its spirit has endured. The kernel of this spirit is that beyond any human judgment, beyond the realms of legal or philosophical decree, human beings—by dint of *being*—are accepted. Just consider what life might be like if we all acknowledged this root condition, if we all acknowledged that we, like everything else, have been selected, and by that very confirmation have been granted a link to all that exists. Jesus seems to be saying that if we begin there, we start to realize how incredible everything is—and not only the source of everything, but our own lives and opportunities to live them out. He further implies that given this realization, there is little reason for us to devalue ourselves, to hate and to brutalize. While, again, such sentiments are ideal, they are also real and have inspired countless transformations throughout time. Consider, for example, how the teaching impacted such initially jaded people as St. Francis of Assisi or, in our day, Thomas Merton; or the addictive personalities in such Christian-inspired self-help groups as Alcoholics Anonymous, Alanon, and Narcotics Anonymous; or those who have benefited in prisons, civil rights movements, and everyday destitution.

In short, the Christian message of unconditional acceptance or love embraces but does not erase the mysterious condition of humanity. As the Protestant theologian Paul Tillich (1952) put it in *The Courage to Be*, we are accepted *in spite of* being "unacceptable" (limited, imperfect, vulnerable). We can trust in the beyond despite a complete ignorance about that which the beyond has in store for us simply because it *is* beyond. Simply because it *is* beyond, God (or Cosmos) becomes a canopy that carries us on the greatest adventure we have ever known—existence itself.

The Awe-Based Paths of the East

While the awe-based paths of the West stress cultivation of the self, those of the East emphasize cultivation of the collective; and whereas the West features the hero-conqueror, the East spotlights the hero-saint. By hero-conqueror, I mean Ambrosio's (2009) "heroes who pursue self-fulfillment," and by hero-saint, I mean heroes who "live for others" (p. 8). These are stereotypes, of course, but they have a resonance in the respective approaches to awe. Whereas Westerners tend to pursue the adventure of living—awe—through personal expression, Easterners tend to pursue these dimensions through the vehicles of family, rulers, or great cosmic processes. To put it another way, while the hero-conqueror participates *personally* in the adventure of living, the hero-saint participates *impersonally* in the adventure of living. On the other hand, both Easterners and Westerners have contributed immeasurably to an awe-based consciousness, and while there is much that sets them apart, there is a great deal that joins them and potentially bridges their interests. We will now deepen these considerations, beginning with our inquiry of the Near East.

Wisdom Teachings of the Near East: Ancient Egypt, India, and Arabia

Egypt
For ancient Egyptians, awe was focused on the afterlife. The humility and wonder—adventure—of living converged on the preparation of the soul for immortal "flight" (Campbell, 1948). As strange as this idea may seem today, it is neither dismissible nor absurd. Who even now can dispute the enigma of death, which converts but does not totally destroy material being. Death may well be another form of life, although it is probably not the form that most of us would readily pursue. Yet in the light of ancient hardships, death certainly had its attractions, even among the most privileged of society.

In the Egyptian *Book of the Dead,* the deceased were accorded a particularly exalted status. Not only was the deceased (usually a pharaoh) equated with Osiris, ruler of the afterlife, but he or she was also mummified and lavishly adorned. The mummification served the purpose, ironically, of preserving the soul while housed in the body, and the adornment served as both protection from evil and offerings to the gods (Garraty & Gay, 1972).

Following the extensive preparations, the deceased is carried through a series of "chapters" or stages. Such stages include the "Chapter of Giving a Mouth to Osiris N ("N" standing for the particular name of the deceased), the "Chapter of Beating Back the Crocodile," and so on. These chapters stand for various actions requested by the deceased, such as the request to be able to open his/her mouth and to "beat back" the evil crocodile from his/her particular part of the underworld. One intriguing request is to "rise out of the egg into the hidden land," which is basically translated as the "idea of death as rebirth," according to Campbell (1948, p. 369).

In the culminating stages, the deceased moves toward increasing identification with Osiris and ultimately to Ra himself. In the chapter "Driving Away the Slaughterings which are Performed in the Underworld" the deceased proclaims that the parts of his or her body are those of various gods. To wit: "My hair is the hair of Nu. My face is the face of the Disk. My eyes are the eyes of Hathor...My neck is the neck of the Divine goddess Isis" and so on (p. 371). The passage concludes: "There is no member of my body that is not the member of some God. The god Thoth shieldeth my body altogether and, and I am Re [the alternative spelling of "Ra"] day by day. I shall not be dragged back by the arms, and none shall lay violent hold upon my hands..." (p. 371).

In the culminating chapters, the deceased and "universal being are known to be one: 'I am Yesterday, Today, and Tomorrow, and I have the power to be born a second time; I am the divine hidden soul who createth the gods...'" (p. 372). Following a final purification of his or her soul, the deceased moves into the "Chapter of Living Nigh to Re," the "Chapter of Causing a Man to Come Back to See his House Upon Earth," the "Chapter of Making Perfect the Soul," and the "Chapter of Sailing in the Great Sun-Boat of Re" (p. 373).

While this *elaborate* system of stages (which echoes later spiritual tracts such as *The Tibetan Book of the Dead*), can be seen as a denial as well as an embrace of the mystery of being, there is little doubt that it evokes awe. The awe in my view is not so much in the explanations but in the *explorations* of a completely enigmatic phase of existence. Hence, we still have something to learn from *The Book of the Dead*— if not from its literal depictions, then from its courageous inquiries.

Similarly, we also have something to learn from the grandeur of the Egyptian pyramids. The Great Pyramid at Giza, for example, remains, at 480 feet in height and 756 feet long, one of the largest buildings in the world. It took some 100,000 laborers and approximately 2.3 million two-and-a-half-ton limestone blocks to erect the structure, which was completed in sweltering desert heat (Garraty & Gay, p. 73). What could have been the motivation for this monumental undertaking? No doubt, the narcissism of the pharaohs and requirements of forced labor had something to do with it, but that does not explain the structure's exquisite craftsmanship and ultimate magnificence. Nor does it explain the general cultural support for the undertaking (Garraty & Gay, 1972). However, what does at least partially explain these facts is the linkage among pyramid, pharaoh, and afterlife. The pyramid was like a resplendent space capsule housing the dreams and hopes of a populace, led by their "great god," the pharaoh. Without these linkages the common people appeared to be destitute, lacking a sense of worth, and bereft of meaning; however, with these linkages they could feel like more than mere observers; they could feel like participants—or "passengers"—in the unparalleled journey of existence. In short, they could become the privileged allies of God.

In sum, then, the ancient Egyptian worldview offers illuminating glimpses into peoples' highest motivations to live. Although its focus is on the afterlife and the pharaohs' ascent into the infinite, its intimation is that all can participate, at some level, in this trek, and that all would be better off to experience that participation, and to prioritize it in one's life.

The Stars of India: Hinduism and Buddhism

By the sixth century B.C.E., ancient India became dominated by a new religious order that sought "salvation from [the] bondage of the material world" (Garraty & Gay, p. 101). This order, inspired by the last section of the Veda called the Upanishads, formed the bedrock of what is now conceived as contemporary Hinduism (p. 101). The essence of Hinduism is renunciation—not renunciation in the sense of self-resignation but in the sense of self-liberation (Smith, 1991). Put another way, the path to awe in Hinduism is the withdrawal or renunciation of self. Through such withdrawal—or "getting out of one's own way"—one is exposed to the "more" of living (Smith, p. 17). This "more" opens one to the follies of living purely for pleasure or for material gain and, alternatively, points one to the infinite possibilities of self–cosmic union.

Within the Hindu tradition there are four basic paths to renunciation, all rooted in the practice of yoga. The term "yoga" derives from the same root as the English term "yoke." Yoga, therefore, connotes a "yoking together" or "integration" of the self with existence (Smith, p. 27). By practicing techniques of yoga, such as carefully crafted body postures and methods of breathing, the Hindu adept was able to experience a sense of union with God or the infinite. As part of this yogic path, the adept also learned to "disidentify" with the various parts of him or her self, and to become one, to the extent possible, with the being that underlies all these parts. Although the paths to yogic transformation are to some extent varied, they all converge on the amazement—serenity, blessedness—of being without discernable boundaries. A yogic master named Sri Nisargadatta Maharaj provided the best and most succinct summary of this worldview that I have seen:

> Give up all questions except one: "Who am I?" After all, the only fact you are sure of is that you are. The "I am" is certain. The "I am this" is not. Struggle to find out what you are in reality.
>
> To know what you are you must first investigate what you are not.
>
> Discover all that you are not—body, feelings, thoughts, time, space, this or that—nothing, concrete or abstract, which you perceive can be you. The very act of perceiving shows that you are not what you perceive.
>
> The clearer you understand that on the level of mind you can be described in negative terms only, the quicker you come to the end of your search and realize that you are the limitless being. (Maharaj, 1973, p. xxii)

The Hindu path then, opens one to the humility and wonder—adventure—of living. It does so through the hard-won art of relinquishment, as distinct from mastery, which is the Western path. However, either of these paths can become distorted as we have seen, and the route to their distortion is dogma and polarization, where no competing perspectives are entertained.

Beginning in the latter part of the sixth century B.C.E., Buddhism was the purported cure for polarized forms of Hinduism. In the hands of Guatama Buddha, the founder of that tradition, words like "absolute" and "Brahman" were viewed as pointers to the ultimate, rather than equations with the ultimate. Although the Buddha agreed with many of the goals of ancient Hindu practice, he found the means to attain those goals wanting in some respects. Among these means was a tendency of some of his Hindu forebears to stress an authoritarian class structure, mechanical ritual, extreme asceticism, and magical fixes in the attainment of samadhi or enlightened self-dissolution. On the other hand, the Buddha developed a philosophy that emphasized egalitarianism, spontaneous attunement, and social compassion. He called his approach to enlightenment the Eight-Fold Path. Without belaboring the details of this path, suffice it say that it advises profound shifts in the way people perceive. In the first path, The Right Views, the student is introduced to the The Four Noble Truths—that life is suffering, that the cause of this suffering is desire (attachment), that this cause can be overcome through mindful nonattachment, and that there are specific methods (the Eightfold Path) that facilitate mindful non-attachment. In the second through eighth paths, intent, speech, conduct, livelihood, effort, mindfulness, and concentration are described and elaborated as stages to liberation. By liberation (or enlightenment), Buddha meant neither perfection nor knowledge of all things. He appropriated things that could be done through human ingenuity to humanity, and things that exceeded it to the unknown.

> "And what have I explained?" Buddha challenged his disciples: "Suffering have I explained, the cause of suffering, the destruction of suffering, and the path that leads to the destruction of suffering have I explained. For this is useful. Therefore, my disciples consider as unexplained what I have not explained....For these things tend not toward edification." (Smith, 1986, p. 143)

This humble stance enabled Buddha to discover an awe-filled universe, replete with sensations, images, and thoughts that continually transformed—and potentially transfixed--all who witnessed them.

Buddhism's vision has achieved remarkable worldwide application. Although it is true that Buddhism, too, can lapse into polarizing rigidity on occasion: consider, for example, Buddha's abandonment of his family on his path to "liberation," or attestations of spiritual bypassing in some Buddhist and other Eastern mystical communities (e.g., Kramer & Alstad, 1993).[7] On the whole, however, Buddhism has shown itself to be a remarkably ethical tradition (Smith, 1986).

Arabia and The Promise of Islam

Islam began with the epiphanies of the prophet Muhammad in 610 C.E. These revelations, which were eventually compiled in a cherished book—the Quran, shattered the moribund traditions of Arabic hierarchy, injustice, and cultural disunity (Armstrong, 2002). Drawing on what he perceived as divine illumination, Muhammad decreed that all people derived from the lineage of Abraham—including Jews, Christians, and Muslims (as they were now called)—owed their allegiance to one God, and not to any substitutes, human or otherwise. This refusal to worship human-made deities (or idols) led Muhammad to preach an egalitarian worldview, where tolerance for those with different beliefs, and compassion for the vulnerable were emphasized. The Quran underlined this approach:

> Do not argue with the followers of earlier revelation otherwise than in a most kindly manner—unless it be such of them as are bent on evil-doing—and say: "We believe in that which has been bestowed from on high upon us, as well as that which has been bestowed upon you; for our God and

---

[7] The traditional explanation for Buddha's abandonment of his wife and young son is that to attain enlightenment one must be impervious to the self or even those close to the self in order to pursue a greater aim: the healing of humanity. However, the highly contentious question remains: whether abandoning one's family—and in particular a dependent child—is a necessary price for enlightenment. There is no ready answer here, and yet a "both/and" approach to the family might, in hindsight, have been a worthy consideration.

your God is one and the same, and it is unto him that we [all] surrender ourselves." (p. 10)

At the same time that the Quran highlighted commonalities among the three Abrahamic faith traditions, as well as those within the Arab community that had splintered off, the Quran also outlawed those aspects of such heritages that had devalued and fragmented their communities. In Mecca, for example, the place where Muhammad experienced his revelation, violence was forbidden, pilgrims were prohibited from carrying arms during the yearly spiritual pilgrimage called the hajj, and all were proscribed from killing even an insect or uttering an angry word (p.11). The Quran viewed war, moreover, as such a "catastrophe" that it pressed Muslims to employ every means necessary to avoid it (p.22). Despite all these differences with the traditions of the past, however, Muhammad's approach attempted to distill the essential wisdom of these traditions, just as Jesus's teaching both departed from and attempted to emulate the core of Jewish prophesy.

To the extent that Islam promoted tolerance and worldly knowledge, it came to flourish, particularly during the height of the Ottoman empire from roughly the fourteenth through eighteenth centuries. This was a time of expansionism to be sure, but also of comparative peace, innovation, and global influence. On the other hand, there had always been periods when rigidity and intolerance reigned within Islam, and one of these was in the ninth century. This was a time of legalistic interpretations of the Quran, and a sense among some that Islamic culture was losing the spirit of its teachings in its quest for literal exactness (Armstrong, 2002, p. 74).

Enter the mystical practice of Sufism. Sufism opposed the strictness of Quranic literalism and transposed it with something much closer to what they viewed as the spirit of this literalism. This spirit emphasized internal attitudes and not just external rules; openness to altered states of consciousness in the quest for spiritual connection, and appreciation of other paths to the holy (p. 74). "The Sufis...were constantly open to the possibility of new truths," wrote Karen Armstrong (p. 74). "Where the Quran described a God of strict justice, Sufis, such as the great woman ascetic Rabiah (d. 801) spoke of a God of love." (p. 74).

In a concerted sense, then, Sufis distilled Quaranic rules into a spiritual philosophy of moment-to-moment life. They applied love and justice to the mind as well as to the material world, and developed rituals to commemorate the transformation. Among these rituals were the dances of the "whirling dervishes" and various forms of meditation to harness the vitality of mystical union. Assuredly, these meditations captured the humility and wonder, and sense of adventure toward living, -and by the time of the great Sufi mystic Jalal al-Din Rumi (1207–73), they enchanted the Islamic populace.

Consider how Rumi brought Sufi philosophy alive in the following iconic poem:

> This human being is a guest house.
> Every morning a new arrival.
>
> A joy, a depression, a meanness,
> some momentary awareness comes
> as an unexpected visitor.
>
> Welcome and entertain them all!
> Even if they're a crowd of sorrows,
> who violently sweep your house
> empty of its furniture,
> still treat each guest honorably.
> He may be clearing you out
> for some new delight.
>
> The dark thought, the shame, the malice,
> meet them at the door laughing,
> and invite them in.
>
> Be grateful for whoever comes,
> because each has been sent
> as a guide from the beyond.
> (cited in Barks, 1995, p. 109)

What mystics like Rumi taught was that humility and wonder are the base for a revitalized experience of life. This experience approaches the world not in black and white but in many-colored hues. Dark thoughts can coexist with humor and sorrow with joy. People can coexist with differences, and differences can bring growth. This is a lesson repeated over and over again among the leading religious mystics—from Lao Tzu to Buddha to Jesus to Mohammad, and it is a clarion call for our own day, our own polarizing institutions.

The thread that connects this awe-based call is presence—the state of heightened attention. But it is not just heightened attention to that which liberates; it is also a lamp to that which agonizes, and it challenges us to acknowledge both.

Taoism and The Far East

Next, we will consider the wisdom traditions of China and Japan. Again, these are not comprehensive discourses on Eastern philosophy, but snapshots about how to cope with uncertainty.

The seeds of mystery-embracing philosophy in China began with Lao Tzu's *Tao Te Ching* (circa sixth century B.C.E.). In this astounding manifesto, Lao Tzu addresses individual spirituality, social harmony, and the evolution of consciousness (Cleary, 1991, p. 1). Just about everything "Eastern" was touched by this diminuitive volume, and just about every major religious figure drew from its well (Chan, 1963).

The *Tao Te Ching* emphasizes renunciation but it does not preach the renunciatory life. It celebrates smallness—that is, keeping oneself humble—but it does not proscribe against becoming an insightful or worldly human being. By contrast, the *Tao* advocates immersing oneself in the world, experiencing one's passions, and cultivating achievements. It also acknowledges political realities. However, what it does not countenance is over-identification with any of these endeavors. It presses for a kind of "effortless effort" in all one engages. This means that one may do all one can to survive, to accomplish practical tasks, and to develop worldly skills, but that there is a great danger in becoming stuck in these strivings, in confusing one's identity with them, and in refusing to let them go. Consider the following two passages:

> The most submissive thing in the world can ride roughshod over the hardest thing in the world....That is why I know the benefit of resorting to no action. The teaching that uses no words, the benefit of resorting to no action, these are beyond

the understanding of all but a very few in the world. (Lao Tzu, 1963, p. 104)

In the pursuit of learning one knows more every day; in the pursuit of the way one does less every day. One does less and less until one does nothing at all, and when one does nothing at all there is nothing that is undone.
It is always through not meddling that the empire is won. Should you meddle, then you are not equal to the task of winning the empire. (p. 109)

The way of wisdom for the *Tao* is to emulate nature—to watch how flowers blossom and then wither away, to observe the tiger that aggresses only when in need of food or when threatened, and to appreciate the storm that passes into blue sky. Everything in its time, everything in its season proclaims the *Tao*. Another way to put this is that one's "yang" (or involvement) must be balanced by one's "yin" (or abandonment) in order for life to flourish.
There is a wonderful Taoist tale that illustrates the wisdom of this mentality:

Once a upon a time there was a Chinese farmer whose horse ran away, and all the neighbors came around to commiserate that evening. "So sorry to hear your horse ran away. This is most unfortunate." The farmer said, "Maybe." The next day the horse came back bringing seven wild horses with it, and everybody came back in the evening and said "Oh, isn't that lucky. What a great turn of events. You now have eight horses!" And he said "Maybe." The next day his son tried to break one of these horses and ride it but he was thrown, and broke his leg, and they all said, "Oh dear, that's too bad," and he said, "Maybe." The following day the conscription officers came around to conscript people into the army and they rejected his son because he had a broken leg. Again all the people came around and said, "Isn't that great!" And he said, "Maybe." (Watts, 1994, p.157)

The tale of the Chinese farmer eloquently illustrates the equanimity of Taoist practice. While the Chinese farmer recognizes the truth of life's extremes, e.g., its joy as well as sorrow, he does not over identify with them. Instead he abides by these extremes just as he abides by that which can and cannot be controlled. His use of the term "maybe" is akin to the idea that one does what one can to effect positive change (e.g., tame a wild horse), but one also recognizes that events far beyond one's control (e.g., the horse running away) can and will derail all of one's efforts. This is the wisdom, the equanimity, of the "way."

The Zen–Shinto Tradition of Japan
Following its export from China, the radiance and serenity of Buddhism were eloquently modified into a Japanese tradition called Zen. This tradition, drawing partly on Shintoism, has had a lasting impact on Japanese poetry, flower arrangement, gardening, architecture, and the martial arts. It has also had a lasting impact on the cultural emphasis on detail, protocol, and quality of presentation—be that in the dining room, the business meeting, or the family gathering. The chief principles of Zen Buddhism are the relinquishment of individuality, the attunement to details, and the unification with existence. The sensibility of Zen is eloquently illustrated by the arresting summations of Basho (1644–1694), who was one of the great originators of haiku poetry. For Basho, as for twentieth century Zen master Yasutani Haku'un Roshi, Buddha nature "moves briskly in detailed particulars. Whenever, wherever, it is the full presentation …" that must be "savored" (Adams, 2010, pp. 48–49). Basho elaborates that if you want to learn about pine, you should "go to the pine," or "if you want to learn about the bamboo" go "to the bamboo." Otherwise," he writes, "you impose yourself on the object and do not learn" (p. 49). He goes on: "Your poetry issues of its own accord when you and the object have become one—when you have plunged deep enough into the object to see something like a hidden glimmering there" (p. 49).

This attention to detail and forgetting of self is captured vividly in Basho's poems about nature. About his journey to the pine forest, he writes concisely:

Pine Islands, ah!
Oh, Pure Islands, ah!
Pine Islands, ah! (p. 50)

As Basho witnesses green leafy foliage, he exclaims:

So holy:
green leaves, young leaves,
in the sun's light (p. 88)

And as Basho soaks in the presence of a cherry blossom, he notes:

Many many things
they bring to mind—
cherry blossoms!

Through these depictions, Basho brings us into direct contact with our experience, with possibilities, and with life. We are invited to marvel at, and not just monitor, our day-to-day encounters.

Chapter 5

Later Embraces of Mystery
Through History

The Reformation as Emancipation

Martin Luther was as much a titan of human freedom as a tyrant of human depravity. His emancipation from the Catholic Church was a liberation for all who were crushed by her authority. In place of Church doctrine, he brought a new ethic of integrity to worship. Instead of mechanical adherence to rules, Luther encouraged a personal appreciation of Christ's teachings. "To be truly" faithful, according to the Protestant scholar Emil Brunner, one must experience "a movement of the affections in love and trust, and a movement of the will in desire to be an instrument of God's redeeming love" (cited in Smith, 1986, p. 465).

The Protestant revolution, in other words, was an act of the "whole personality" (p. 465). It honored people's needs to internalize God in their own ways, drawing on their own national and personal identities. The basis for the Protestant revolution was trust—a trust that at some basic level, God (or Christ) is good, and that through a person's acceptance of that goodness he or she will also do good in the world. This idea is very close to the Jewish notion, elaborated by Leo Baeck (1987), that appreciation for God's mystery, leads to and authenticates an ethical approach to life.

The Protestant revolution was guided by a concept called the Protestant Principle. This principle, directly relevant to contemporary polarization, states the following: 1) the relative (or human viewpoint) cannot be absolutized (as in Church dogma), and 2) no human or institution is above God (Smith, p. 467). The problem, of course, is who is to define "God" if not human beings. And if this definition becomes too literal—as it has throughout the history not only of Protestantism but of most world religions—then how can it avoid becoming dogmatic in itself? It cannot, as Protestantism has amply demonstrated throughout the ages. Nevertheless, the Protestant *Principle* behind the various expressions of Protestantism was and remains one of the most emancipating shifts in the history of Western religion. Unlike few other religious ideas, it signaled a decided turn away from central authority, be it that of Church or Kingdom, and *toward* individuality. In parallel with the spirit of the Renaissance, it renewed the Socratic ideals of inquiry, deliberation, and personally meaningful truth.

One of the outgrowths of the Protestant revolution was the increasing realization that divinity (or the awesomeness of creation) was accessible to everyone, not just concecrated priests. This realization led to one the most visionary Protestant movements of the Renaissance—Calvinism, named after the mid-sixteenth century Protestant reformer, John Calvin (1509–64). Calvinism was a key constituent of Renaissance life, prizing homelife, work, and even secular scholarship in the same divine light as that previously reserved for clerical elites (Campolo, 2010). For all of its shortcomings, moreover—and it had many—Calvinism also served as a beacon of the new democraticization of spirit, and applied its principles widely.

One of the chief Calvinist teachings was that the exploitation of the material world was not by definition contrary to Christian values, but indeed, could be resonant with those values. The question for Calvinists was not whether one's interests were internal or external but whether they served "heartily...unto the Lord" (Campolo, p. 3). While this philosophy sometimes led to excesses such as the "empty" accumulation of wealth, it also led to the advancement of individuals' standard of living, improvement in the social infrastructure, and preservation of the environment (Campolo, 2010). "Let everyone regard himself as a steward of God," Calvin wrote, and "then he will never conduct himself dissolutely, nor corrupt by abuse those things which God requires to be preserved" (p. 5). Even the physical sciences were viewed favorably by Calvinist adherents, for they "provided insights into the nature and character" of God (p. 4). From these standpoints, then, Calvinism expanded the human capacity to wonder—even in domains traditionally frowned upon by the

Church, such as science—and by so doing expanded the foundation stone for wisdom.

Wisdom Paths of the Enlightenment

The chief focus of the Enlightenment (roughly 1700–1800 C.E.) was rational knowledge (Berlin, 1999; Jones, 1969). Enlightenment thinkers such as Francis Bacon, John Locke, and Marque de Condorcet believed that if human beings worked hard enough, they and not gods, could determine the destiny of humanity. This turning point in human history swung from the passive reliance on faith to the animated reliance on reason to solve daily practical problems. Condorcet elaborated:

> If man can, with almost complete assurance, predict phenomena when he knows their laws...why, then, should it be regarded as a fantastic undertaking to sketch, with some pretense to truth, the future destiny of man on the basis of his history? The sole foundation for belief in the natural sciences is this idea, that the general laws directing the phenomena of the universe, known or unknown, are necessary and constant. (cited in Jones, p. 2)

The openness to reason, to the human being's capacity to discover and to find solutions, was one of the pivotal outgrowths of the Western Renaissance. Although such zealotry could become excessive, as when "reason" overtook perspective, it could also be tremendously emancipating in the hands of those who humbly sculpted their destinies. The scientific method, as it was called, was a remarkable program for noticing and cataloguing the world. It was a bellwether of the miraculous technologies to come, both within and without the human personality.

The range of scientifically grounded innovations just prior to and during the Enlightenment was nothing short of dizzying. This range stretched from the far-reaching expeditions of Portuguese and Spanish explorers, to the advances in medical technology (such as the development of the microscope), to the breakthroughs in physical and astronomical research. It also stretched from the philosophy of mind to the science of human (and animal) development.

Reason and the scientific method also opened new paths for democratically elected governments and egalitarian principles of law. France's "equality, liberty, and fraternity" arose in large part as a result of these developments—and the basis for the Constitution derived in part from the Enlightenment reasoning of of Voltaire, John Stuart Mill, and John Locke.

Karl Marx also drew on Enlightenment reasoning to develop his communist manifesto. Communism, according to Marx, empowered people to live for more than material gain. Through the equalization of income, Marx believed that not only would people be satisfied materially, but they also would be freed to pursue "higher" goals. Among such goals would be the attainment of higher learning, the refinement of a trade, and the contribution to societal well-being.

Enlightenment reasoning, then, enabled both wonder, adventure and analytical constraint. It widened the ability to investigate questions that have dogged humanity since the dawn of time, such as where we came from, what our nature is, and how we should live. But it also stopped short of presuming absolute solutions to those questions. At their best, Enlightenment truths were qualified by available evidence (i.e., sense perceptions) and limits of logic. Following Hume, truths became "probabilities," and propositions "testable" (Berlin, 1999).

Romantic Awe
If the antidote to polarization is the holding of paradox, then Romanticism could be counted as an antidote. "Twice two makes four is not life, gentleman," the great Russian novelist Fyodor Dostoyevsky once exclaimed. "It is the beginning of death" (cited in Kaufmann, 1975, p. 77). The core Romantic vision challenged Enlightenment reason. It was large and it was exhilarating, but it was also mysterious and dark. If the Enlightenment was marked by the calcuable, Romanticism was distinguished by the fathomless. Or to put it in the inimitable terms of twentieth century theologian Paul Tillich (1963b): the "awareness of the infinite in the finite" was the hallmark of Romanticism.

By the late eighteenth century, the stress on Enlightenment reasoning began to crack (Berlin, 1999). Increasingly, people found that the systematization of personal and cultural life led to some grotesque results, such as the pollution of cities, the degradation of nature, and the intellectualization of spirit. In the wake of this disillusionment, an alternative paradigm arose— Romanticism. Whereas the Renaissance and Enlightenment homed in on the strictly rational, Romanticism broke open to the nonrational, the far-ranging and unruly. Just as with the Enlightenment and all other historical phases, these developments sometimes broke down into totalizing obsessions, such as the preoccupation with race or the presumption of greatness. But they also paved the path for a greatly expanded understanding of life.

The roots of romanticism could be seen in early Renaissance art, in the suppleness of a Rembrandt painting or a sculpture by Michelangelo. They could be seen in the mystical musings of a Spinoza or Jacob Boheme, as well as in the folk traditions of Renaissance Spain. The twentieth century Spanish poet Federico Garcia Lorca eloquently captured the latter, as well as the general Romantic temper, with his passage about "duende":

> Everything that has black tones has duende. And there is no truth greater. These black tones are mystery itself whose roots are held fast in the mulch we all know and ignore, but whence we arrive at all that is substantial in art. Black tones...are a mysterious power which everyone feels but no philosopher can explain....I have heard an old guitar teacher say that "the duende is not in the singer's throat, the duende rises inside from the very soles of one's feet." That is to say, it is not a question of ability or aptitude but a matter of possessing an authentic living style; that is to say of blood, of culture most ancient, of creation in art. (cited in Bly, Hillman, & Meade, 1992, p. 165)

The stirrings of Romanticism proper began in Germany following the double upheaval of Lutheranism and the Thirty Years War (1618–1648) (Berlin, 1999). Lutheranism emphasized the power of the individual against the authority of the Church, and the Thirty Years War highlighted the outcry of a decimated German populace. As a result of this outcry, many either retreated into "scholastic pedantry" or, on the contrary, plunged headlong into personal and spiritual inquiry. Many Germans at the time reserved especial animus toward the French (Berlin, 1999, p. 35). The blow dealt by France in the Thirty Years War (and later Napoleonic wars) was not lost on the German populace. This was a populace that already felt like the stepchildren of Europe and was unforgiving toward those, like the Catholic Church, who dictated the terms of their survival.

By the time of the Enlightenment, several German thinkers staged powerful protests against French rationalism—among them Johann Georg Hamann, who rebelled against the Voltairean ideal of a rationally ordered life. Where science and contentment reigned, Hamann argued, the dynamic and creative individual was likely to be lost. The progenitor of the so-called "sturm and drang" ("storm and stress") movement of early German Romanticism, Hamann influenced such scholars as Immanual Kant, Johann von Goethe, and Danish existentialist Soren Kierkegaard.

Although Kant was an Enlightenment thinker, his interrogations of mind led him to the point where Enlightenment rationality could no longer apply. This point in turn inspired his classic distinction between phenomena—the basic structures of rational consciousness—and noumena, the elusive realms of spirit or intuition that transcended conventional consciousness. Goethe became known primarily for his opus magnum, *Faust.* The story of a brilliant but devitalized medieval scholar, *Faust* brings into focus Romanticism's critique of the Enlightenment. Just as the typical Enlightenment philosophe, Faust was a top-heavy individual. His head was filled with book knowledge, but his heart was woefully undernourished. This condition led to some tragic consequences of overreaching, just as the Terror overreached against French propriety. Through its cautionary tone, however, the drama pointed to a maturing Romanticism. This Romanticism acknowledged the full paradoxes of living— our smallness *and* our greatness; our longings and our follies. Kierkegaard (1849/1954), who is in many ways the inspiration of this volume, echoes Goethe's insights. His philosophy of existentialism explicitly embraced humanity's paradoxical condition. The self, he wrote, is a "synthesis of infinitude and finitude, which relates itself to itself, whose task is to become itself" (p. 162). He also wrote that the "gain of infinity is never attained except through despair" (p. 160). For Kierkegaard, as for Goethe, the full human is in part a tragic human, harrowingly constricted and fragile but equally astoundingly resourceful and bold.

On the heels of German Romanticism, and partially influenced by it, England also embarked on a Romantic road. William Blake, Samuel Taylor Coleridge, and William Wordsworth, three of the top representatives of British Romanticism, each portrayed the infinite in the finite in unique and compelling ways. In the "Marriage of Heaven and Hell, for example, Blake (1791/1988) wrote: "Without contraries is no progression. Attraction and Repulsion, Reason and Energy, Love and Hate, are necessary to Human existence" (pp. 66–67). He also wrote in the same poem that "If the doors of perception were cleansed every thing would appear as it is, infinite. For man has closed himself up, till he sees all things thro' narrow chinks of his cavern" (p.73). Coleridge looked profoundly through those chinks and found what he termed "multeity in unity" (Kirschner, 1996, p. 162). Drawing in part from the German Romantic tradition, multeity in unity referred to the unity in which mind and nature fit together and yet remain distinct (p. 162). It also referred to the "higher order" unities, such as in mystical states, in which the mind or subject achieves increasing harmony with nature (Kirschner, 1996). With Wordsworth, nature became an even livelier arena within which to "play." In his classic *Prelude* he pens:

Not in Utopia, subterraneous Fields,
Or some secreted Island, Heaven knows where!
But in the very world which is the world
Of all of us, the place in which, in the end,
We find our happiness, or not at all. (p. 165)

The point to be aware of in Romantic tradition is that so-called religious states of mind, such as faith, connection, and existential love, are all achievable without formalized religious doctrine. This "natural supernaturalism" is a defining moment in Western intellectual history and sets the stage for a third ideological path—that *between* rationality and faith (Abrams, 1973).

In Russia, too, we find some of the most sparkling examples of this Romantic blend. Dostoyevsky's *Notes from Underground* (1864) was a clarion call for the expansion of personal and social vision. In a bellow against mathematical precision in human decision-making, Dostoyevsky proclaims:

> ...who knows...perhaps the only goal on earth to which mankind is striving lies in [the] incessant process of attaining and not in the thing to be attained, which must always express itself as a formula, as positive as twice two makes four. [But] such positiveness is not life, gentleman,...it is the beginning of death. (cited in Kaufmann, 1975, p. 77)

Leo Tolstoy pointed to this sensibility in his *Death of Ivan Ilych*, in which a sedentary bureaucrat suddenly discovers he has a fatal cancer that gives him only months to live. As he descends deeper into his illness, he pauses to reflect on how he has lived—how much of it he spent on idle chatter, robotic routines, and futile gestures. At the same time, however, he becomes increasingly aware of even the briefest pleasures of his present life—such as his youthful servant's exuberance, the love for his family, and the animated memories of childhood. At one point he "explains" his situation by invoking the tired logical syllogism that "Caius is a man, all men are mortal, therefore Caius [and he himself] is mortal" (Tolstoy, 1886/1960, p. 131). But then he realizes the falseness of this comparison, just as he realizes the falseness of the abstractions he clung to much of his life. He realizes that

> he was not Caius, not an abstract man, but a creature quite, quite separate from all others. He had been little Vanya, with a mama and a papa, with Mitya and Volodya, with the toys, a coachman and a nurse...with all the joys, griefs, and delights of childhood, boyhood, and youth. What did Caius know of the smell of that striped leather ball Vanya had been so fond of? Had Caius kissed his mother's hand like that and did the silk of her dress rustle so for Caius? Had he rioted like that at school when the pastry was bad? Had Caius been in love like that?....Caius really was mortal, and it was right for him to die; but for me, little Vanya, Ivan

Ilych, with all my thoughts and emotions, it's altogether a different matter. (p. 132)

This is a cry, a great wail for the depth and richness of a human life. It is perhaps one of the most touching wails in the history of literature, and points to one overarching theme—the appreciation for life's subtleties, for the places it doesn't "resolve," and for its almost intolerable, aching beauty, particularly against the backdrop of death.

In late nineteenth century America, the Great Awakening of religion and Enlightenment rationality came together in the neo-romantic vision called Transcendentalism. Led by such luminaries as Ralph Waldo Emerson, Henry David Thoreau, and Walt Whitman, transcendentalism combined Unitarian ecumenicism, Calvinist personalism, and Platonic idealism to forge a new life philosophy (Nichols, 2006, p. 5). This life philosophy countenanced neither calculative science nor absolutist theology but steered an inspired course between them. That course, loosely speaking, was an attempt to found a democratic spirituality, a nature-loving personalism, and a just and hopeful world. In his classic essay "Nature," Emerson sounded the transcendentalist tone:

> The stars awaken a certain reverence, because though always present they are inaccessible; but all natural objects make a kindred impression, when the mind is open to their influence. Nature never wears a mean appearance. Neither does the wisest man extort her secret, and lose his curiosity by finding out all her perfection. Nature never becomes a toy to a wise spirit. (Emerson, 1836/1992, p. 5)

In the passage above, Emerson hits on all three transcendental chords—personal religiosity (or spirituality), reverence for the natural world, and caretaking of the planet. Whitman takes these themes a step further with his acknowledgement of the paradoxes inherent in each: life is not always fair, personal, or loving, but the challenge is to embrace it nonetheless.

"Do I contradict myself," wrote Whitman in *Leaves of Grass*, "Very well then....I contradict myself; I am large....I contain multitudes" (Whitman, 1855/1959, p. 85). He goes on:

> Great is goodness; I don't know what it is any more than I know what health is....but I know it is great. Great is wickedness....I find I often admire it as much as I admire goodness; Do you call that a paradox? It certainly is a paradox. The eternal equilibrium of things is great, and the eternal overthrow of things is great. And there is another paradox..." (p. 145)

One is reminded here of Coleridge's "multeity in unity," and indeed, Coleridge, as with other Romantics, was a notable influence on transcendental thinkers. Yet Whitman and Thoreau in particular brought a certain earthiness to "big-picture" thinking that exemplified a peculiarly American style. Consider Thoreau's thoughts on solitude:

> I find it wholesome to be alone in the greater part of the time. To be in company, even with the best, is soon wearisome and dissipating. I love to be alone. I never found the companion that was so companionable as solitude. (Thoreau, 1854, p. 119)

At the same time, consider what Thoreau said about civil disobedience and the obligation to stand up for social justice:

> I do not hesitate to say, that those who call themselves Abolitionists should at once effectually withdraw their support, both in person and property, from the government of Massachusetts, and not wait till they constitute a majority of one....I think that it is enough if they have God on their side, without waiting for that other one. Moreover, any man more right than his neighbors constitutes a majority of one already. (Thoreau, http://thoreau.eserver.org/civil2.html)

What we see here is that transcendental thinkers like Thoreau did not hesitate to engage in a full life, a full experience, and a full appraisal of the adversaries to that life and experience. There is nothing "neat" about their worldviews; they are not stitched together like so many machine-cut yarns of thread, but they are alive, insightful, and anchored in real-life perplexities.

Toward an Awe-Based Democracy

The quest for a full life, a dynamic and diversified life, was the chief aspiration of eighteenth century democracy. Despite its grounding in Enlightenment rationality, the early democracy movements in Europe and the United States also gave vent to Romantic stirrings in music, painting, and literature. Reason, ironically, led to the acceptance of nonrational modes of expression, which in turn expanded what had become "reasonable." One way to conceive of this evolution is the shift from technical to "ecstatic" reason (Tillich, 1963a, p. 53), or Enlightenment rationality to romantic realism.

The issue here was not to rest on one polarity of thought—e.g., reason or sentiment—but to acknowledge the truth–value of both. It was in this atmosphere that Kierkegaard forged his synthesis of finite and infinite self, and that Goethe, in *Faust,* united vitality with caution. While excesses of either mechanical rationality or unbridled passion abounded, the enduring works of modernity incorporated elements of both. "The heart has reasons," seventeenth century philosopher Blaise Pascal (1654/1991, p. 41) succinctly uttered, "that reason knows not;" and the reverse could also be said, to equivalent effect.

Another major contributor to this point of view was America's premier philosopher and founding psychologist, William James. With his work on "pragmatism," James (1907/1963) combined the radical openness of Romanticism with the practical discernment of Enlightenment rationality. For James, the issue of validity (or "truth") hinged not on some cerebral logic, or even on concrete sense perception, but on the consequence of the experience. This pragmatic criterion for truth opened science up to the profoundly personal as well as the publically verifiable, the qualitative as well as the quantitative, and even the artistic and religious, as well as the institutional and academic. The question was: Does the experience "work" for the party or parties affected? Who benefits, and is their benefit justified in the marketplace of deliberation? This Romantic–

Rationalist mix became the hallmark of a new democratic spirit, a spirit of tradition and innovation combined.

It is from this paradoxical view that we cannot overlook the influence of African American gospel (or "the old negro spiritual," as Martin Luther King put it) on democratic life. Although the White church was traditionally a place of staid conformity, the African American gospel church of the late eighteenth century was a rollicking exception. Drawing from African tribal traditions as well as local culture, the early African American church steered a delicate path. On one hand, it provided a place of sanctuary for pious worshipers, but on the other hand, it furnished an outlet for passions and rage. This path between socially accepted piety and sublimated revolt formed the basis not only for such musical movements as black gospel, and later in varying degrees, jazz, rhythm and blues, and rock and roll; it also helped to inspire such social movements as the abolition of slavery, the emancipation of women, the civil rights and free speech movements, and myriad movements in between (Carson, 1998; Zinn, 2003).

The encouragement to express oneself with abandon—to sing, to move, and to emote and yet cleave to decorum—was yet another basis for a new democratic and uniquely American folk wisdom. This wisdom emphasized a humanism that shortchanged neither body nor spirit, individuality nor community in their concordance with intellect. Indeed, it could be said that many of the holistic healing movements of the 1950s and 1960s were traceable in part to gospel spirituality. Among these were the Beat philosophy, mind/body therapies, and New Age spirituality. The convergence of these movements with the pragmatic and transcendentalist movements discussed earlier, as well as with parallel intellectual movements in existential and humanistic philosophy, cleared the way for a seismic change in day-to-day life. The take-home message of this change was that life could be affirmed in spite of and, in many cases, in light of the oppressive conditions that threatened it; and that beyond affirmation, life could also be enriched, deepened, and expanded on the basis of this new sensibility—humility and wonder toward the world.

Real-World Trends: Nones, Occupy, and Arab Spring

While there are no sure signs of an awe-based, fluidly centered reform in today's world, there are some hints that such a reform could be starting. The so-called "Nones" movement in the world of religion and the "Occupy Wall Street" and "Arab Spring" movements in politics have elements that embrace a new, more flexible path. The Nones are "the fastest-growing religious demographic," now comprising about 12% of the U.S. population and an even higher percentage, about a quarter, of younger Americans (Weiner, 2011, December 19). What strikes me about the Nones is that they exhibit qualities of elasticity and depth in the world of religion that defy polarizing extremes. For example, although they're quite spiritual and open to divinity, Nones refuse to affiliate with any major religion or sect. They also appreciate exploration and experimentation with religious traditions but without buying into their dogma. "Nones don't get hung up on whether a religion is 'true,'" Eric Weiner (2011) wrote in a recent column in the New York Times, "instead [they] subscribe to William James's maxim that 'truth is what works.' If a certain spiritual practice makes us better people—more loving, less angry—then it is necessarily good, and by extension 'true'" (p. 2). This pragmatic view of religiosity is also reflective of the Nones' take on atheism—the question is not what some authority declares is absolutely unshakable, but what people experience intimately, within and among themselves, and how this awareness impacts their day-to-day lives. Weiner put it this way:

> What we need is someone...who can invent not a new religion, but a new way of being religious....this new way would be straightforward and unencumbered and absolutely intuitive. Most important, it would be highly interactive. I imagine a religious space that celebrates doubt, encourages experimentation and allows one to utter God without embarrassment. A religious operating system for the Nones among us. (p. 2)

On a parallel front, the Occupy Wall Street movement also shows signs of fluidly centered, awe-based thinking. Although in its nascence, the Occupy Wall Street movement is both a protest and an affirmation of a more ethical approach to life. It is a protest against the greed and amorality of capitalism (the so-called "one percent"), and it is an affirmation of the importance of community responsibility, just and equitable working conditions, and educational opportunities for the disadvantaged (the so-called "ninety-nine percent"). Further, Occupy Wall Street is neither a regional movement nor confined to any one sector of corporate domination. It is a world movement that embraces quality of life, alongside basic material subsistence. The Occupy Wall Street movement, moreover, does not seem to be *against* capitalism, which has improved life for many people, so much as *for* a more moral and just capitalism, a kind of capitalist equivalent of the Nones. What all this means, according to Lisa Duggan, a professor of social and cultural analysis at New York University is that Occupy Wall Street "needs to be seen in the broader context" of other movements, such as "the Arab Spring," that do not seek to replace so much as augment and update established practices (Buckley, 2012, p. 18).

The Arab Spring movement began in Tunisia in December 2010. Soon afterward, Egypt, and then Libya and Yemen, fell under its explosively liberating spell. The Arab Spring was (and is) a revolt against absolute monarchy, human rights violations, government corruption, and economic decline in each of the nations it has impacted, which now include many other Arab and even Israeli territories. While the essential philosophy of the Arab Spring has yet to be defined, there are several noteworthy attributes relevant to awe-based democracy. Each of these derive from the so-called "Turkish model" and include *secularization*, or the desire for increased separation between civil and religious authority; *democracy*, or the framework for free and fair elections and a constitution to protect civil and human rights; *political Islam*, or the establishment of a moderate Islamic government, and economic liberalizaiton, or the expansion of free markets and trade (see *The Economist*, 2011). Allegedly, the most influential philosophy of the Turkish Model is from a religious teacher named Fethullah Gulen. Gulen "mixes the vocabulary of Sufism with language that is broadly pro-business and pro-democracy" (http://www.economist.com/node/21525408). Put succinctly, the Turkish Model represents a liberal democracy informed by Islamic values.

Perhaps the most prominent contemporary example of the influence of the Turkish Model is the newly revised platform of the Muslim Brotherhood Party of Egypt. In theory, this platform avoids fundamentalist Sharia law, but explicitly embraces Islamic values in its advocacy of expanded liberalization and democracy. As of this writing, however, the question as to whether the Muslim Brotherhood can actually deliver what it now advocates is very much an open one.

Despite all their challenges, the upshot of the Arab Spring—as well as Nones and Occupy movements—is that they point to a new possibility of life among diverse and aspiring peoples. They point to a time when the sacred and the secular can inform one another, temper one another's rigidities as well as excesses, and enlarge one another's capacity for deepening and enriching life.

Coda

The conclusion of this review is that the power centers of history contain within them the seeds of great wisdom and beauty alongside their ghastly records of one-sidedness. One cannot simply say that a Germany or Russia—or for that matter, France, Britain, or the United States—is reducible to an imperious beast any more than one can say an India, China, or Japan is comparable to a glorious beacon. Humanity is shot through with compensatory brutality, but it also realizes pliability, deliberation, and awe. The road to these qualities is obviously not a simple one, but it is available—just as the "mistake" of polarization is perpetually reversible.

If there is one thread that runs through the polarization–paradox matrix, it is not that individuals or cultures avoid excess. It is that wise individuals and cultures operate less on panic and more on vision, less by compulsion and more by choice, less by desperation and more by aspiration (see also Prilleltensky, 2006). The result is that like Washington at Mt. Vernon, or King at Montgomery, they sense when to burst forth and when to pull back, when to revolutionize and when to temper, and when to assert and when to defer. This is the lesson of the embrace of mystery throughout history. And it is the take-home message of the power centers worldwide when they *empower* as opposed to crush.

Chapter 6

Toward A Fluid Center Of Life

The embrace of mystery throughout history has brought us to a very critical juncture. How can we limit polarization *today* and move toward a society based more on awe than on panic, choice more than on compulsion, and depth more than on mechanical routine? Or, to put it another way, how can we limit polarization without devolving into either numbing indifference or muddled moderation?

First of all, we need to address childrearing. If we don't get that right, the roots of polarized minds will ever elude us. In this vein, we need to enable workable doses of anxiety as well as wonder into the developmental mix. In my view, the mistake we have made repeatedly in recent Western culture is that to counteract the ill-effects of the deprived and punitive social environments of our past, we shamelessly ratchet up the pristine and sanitizing capabilities of our technocratic present. That has not worked very well. At best we produce kids who feel a modicum of esteem for themselves but who later, in the face of life's trials, tend to flail or just simply "get by." At worst, we see kids who just capsize in the wake of such illusion-shattering trials, and who withdraw, self-mutilate, or even commit suicide as a result. In order to counter these calamities, we need to appreciate that living a full life means living a venturesome life, and that entails uncovering anxieties as well as consoling conveniences.

In a nutshell, we need to enable children to experience the *daunting* as well as the comforting on their evolving paths. By daunting I mean intimidating and challenging more than overwhelming and disabling (although I recognize that the latter occur from time to time in every life). I certainly do not advocate purposeful discouragement in children's lives. However, what I do mean is that if a kid is sad or mad, let him *be* sad or mad for a time; help him deal with the feeling but not through incessant diversions, fixes, or denials. Help him deal with the feelings by talking them through as he's ready or to the extent possible, working them through by himself. There is nothing easy or linear about these recommendations, I realize that I neither can nor desire to "tell" people what to do with their children (short of advising against serious harm). But what I do attempt here is to sketch a certain atmosphere, a certain temper, that the present study and my own life experience suggest.

For example, many kids today experience quick highs, virtual thrills, and numbing entertainments. But how many times do they experience (or are supported to experience) the solemnity of a painting, the wonder of a storm, or the puzzlement of a death? How often are they encouraged to play in fields, splash in mud, or wrestle over great books? How often are they encouraged to notice—to really taste their food, to check in with how they and others feel, to see how people treat one another, and to witness how a variety of people live? While it is true that some of these challenges are luxuries from an economic point of view—e.g., the ability to travel, obtain great food, become educated, etc.—many others can be creatively cultivated in just about any circumstances. The question is, will parents and teachers step up to the task of supportively nourishing whole-bodied experiences of life? Or will we continue to cater to part-processes of life, such as those that pertain soley to the appetites, or to the fashionable, or to the formulaic?

I and others have suggested elsewhere that to be vibrant and vital education needs to immerse kids in disciplined, communal, *and* solitary activities. These activities bring them alive, intrigue them, and sometimes shake their worlds (Becker, 1967; Schneider, 2004). For example, give them classes on how cultures have become both alienated and awe inspired throughout history. Challenge them to turn those findings toward their own lives. Help them look at how belief and behavior in ancient Egypt pertains to what kids believe and do today. Aid them to see what's missing from today's lifestyle that was appreciated by the ancient Chinese. Support them to consider what can be borrowed and updated from the early Greeks, Hindus, or Christians. Challenge them to consider what lessons can be learned from the French Terror, the Soviet revolution, or the Nazi "Final Solution." In other areas, enlist kids to engage the power of science or literature through collaborative projects, field studies, and classic books and films. Encourage them to emulate the steps of great thinkers through experiments, self-created plays, and dialogues. These are the gateways, the awe-based alternatives to the denial, half-thinking, and half-living on which so much of traditional education has been forged. To be sure, there will always be blind spots in the new curricula, but the key is to be more aware of those blind spots, to grapple with them, and even to experience a healthy respect for them.

Part of what we're aiming at here is to help kids (and also adults) build a revitalizing meta-narrative. This meta-narrative both acknowledges the status quo—e.g., the pain, the perks, and the necessities of conventional living —but also expands out to the really mega-story that far exceeds what we are typically told. This great "untold" story (or internalization) begins with the parents or caretakers who are aware of it themselves, who exhibit being in touch with it through their own trials, and who share it with their children through diverse channels.

Self-Esteem
The meta-narrative to which I refer here is basic acceptance. But it is not acceptance deriving strictly from a person, family, or culture. Rather, it is acceptance that derives from life, from existence itself. The truth that these carriers of the meta-narrative convey is that, for reasons unknown, *we have all been chosen to live.* This simple fact means not that we are all inherently "good" or "moral" or "superior;" but that we are all inherently *worthy.* We are all inherently worthy of being a participant in the greatest, most radical venture ever known, and that is life. In all frankness, we really have no idea what this life or existence holds in store for us or what it will ultimately accomplish. But what we can know *emphatically* is that no matter what we look like, think, or achieve, we are all at bottom acceptable, and no lover, leader, tribe, nationality, religion, icon, or idol can ever take that away from us.

So there we have it: In an awe-based, fluidly centered society, caretakers will help us to see that, from the start, we all have self-esteem. They will help us to see that by the very nature of our participation in existence we are elevated—we are embraced. And while some may continue to devalue this existential realization, e.g., by relegating it to physical or energetic "processes," or by casting it as absurd, what they cannot deny, and what the carriers of the meta-narrative will continue to advocate, is that no matter what skeptics say existence is still amazing; it is unending, and it defies encapsulation.

Hence, the self-esteem and, in turn, polarization problem is not a simple matter of conveying to kids that they are natural, evolutionary processes acting in concert with other such processes, or that they are "good" when they contribute to human adaptation. Rather, it is a matter of embodying and illuminating participatory awe. It is a matter of letting kids in on peoples' puzzlements, peoples' struggles with the world. But it is also about apprising kids of peoples' connection with the world—their ways of appreciating even the groundlessness upon which we all sway, and of negotiating that groundlessness in ritual and celebration, inquiry and contemplation.

With a base in awe-informed self-esteem, kids, in my view, are less likely to turn against themselves or others, less likely to act out or to cover over their feelings with drugs or pretense, and less likely to divert themselves with frivolities. Conversely, they are more likely to develop the capacity to love, to value while remaining curious about themselves and others, and to grapple with life's perplexities. When they become adults, these kids are in an optimal position to support their culture's psychospiritual growth, alongside of and in light of its material accomplishments. To use extravagant examples, they are more inclined to mirror Einstein, who achieved great professional mastery but not at the expense of concern for the welfare of the planet; or Eleanor Roosevelt, who excelled at political craft while remaining sensitive to her fellow citizens.

On a more ordinary scale, kids with awe-informed self-esteem are more likely to mature into the manager of the grocery store who is genuinely interested in the food that it offers, who presses to find out about that food, to feel comfortable with its origins, to take pride in its nutritional and aesthetic value. These kids are more likely to turn into the boss who is willing to hold periodic meetings with his or her employees to find out how they feel about their job, what aspirations they have for their job, and what the job means in the bigger picture of their lives and communities. Such kids are more likely to grow into bankers, real estate developers and pharmaceutical manufacturers who look beyond their strict profit margins and consider the larger communities within which they operate. They are more likely to care about their impact on the environment, on the personal lives of the people they serve, and on the implications of their work for the cultural and political conditions of humanity. These awe-informed kids are more likely to grow into the religious leader who emphasizes the generosity of his or her religious faith, who reaches out to other faiths, creeds, and even ideologies in the co-creation of his or her "living" tradition. This is the leader who is open to co-celebrations, rituals, and dialogues in the affirmation of spirit, and who actively encourages the dispersal of such generosity in the machinations of the secular world. Finally, such awe-grounded kids are more likely to become the politician who prizes personal encounters concerning issues of moral import, right along with conventional processes of deliberation. This is the kind of politician who submits his or her agenda to the test of deep personal and interpersonal inquiry prior to the execution of laws, and who calls for the parallel spirit of deep democracy in the constituents for whom they serve. Would such a politician be more likely to lead a just and equitable society? I have little doubt. (See *Rediscovery of Awe* [Schneider, 2004] and *Awakening to Awe* [Schneider, 2009] for an elaboration of these proposals.)

    In short, the result of all this is that an awe-based reformation would begin to impact every sector of society and potentially the world. The consequent effects of such reformation would be a strengthening of *appreciation*—appreciation for the origins of life and existence, appreciation for the wisdom of tradition, and appreciation for the development of new wisdoms and new adaptations based partially on the past but also, and not trivially, on the spontaneity and gravity of the moment. These changes require a facile new mind—a mind (and heart) that can sense the awe-based beneath every human breath and that can keep in touch with that grounding, draw upon it, and translate it into life actions. To be sure, I *may* be speaking of an impossible utopian world here, but I don't think so. I think many people already know exactly what I'm elaborating and are beginning to apply it to their own lives. These people know what it means to sense the exhilaration of existence in countless and subtle ways—through a face, a touch, and a word, let alone through the miracle of a seascape, birth, or invention. They know that our collective challenge is to follow up on these life-awakening gems, gather them, cherish them, and prioritize them in the struggle for a rejuvenated world.

In Nietzsche's description of Goethe, we have all the ingredients we need:

> Goethe sought help from history, natural science, antiquity, and also Spinoza, but above all, from practical activity; he surrounded himself with limited horizons; he did not retire from life but put himself into the midst of it; he was not fainthearted but took as much as possible upon himself, over himself, into himself. What he wanted was *totality*; he fought the extraneousness of reason, senses, feeling, and will....*He disciplined himself to wholeness* [emphasis mine]....
>
> Goethe conceived a human being who...might dare to afford the whole range and wealth of being natural, being strong enough for such freedom; the [person] of tolerance, not from weakness but from strength....
>
> Such a spirit who has *become free* stands amid the cosmos with a joyous and trusting fatalism, in the *faith* that only the particular is loathsome, and that all is redeemed in the whole. (Nietzsche, 1889/1982, p. 554)

Epilogue

The Take-Home Messages

It is now time to put together what we know. And what do we know? We know that one alternative to polarization is the acknowledgement of life's paradoxes—our smallness and greatness, humility and possibility before creation. These paradoxes keep us in constant check both personally and collectively. Our smallness, for example, ever apprises us of the danger of growing too big—of arrogance and of overstepping our resources; and our greatness ever alerts us from cutting ourselves too short—of becoming petty, narrow, or grievously repressed. We see the consequences of these paradoxical realizations every time a leader or society demurs from quick and easy proclamations, dehumanization of adversaries, and savagery of attack; we also see it in the choice for understanding vs. presumption, inquiry vs. dogma, and deliberative, impassioned encounter vs. decree. On the other hand, we see the consequences of ignoring the paradoxical every time a leader or society presumes to be inviolable, lords themselves over others, and crushes their adversaries. We also see the consequences every time the victims of such outrages become outrageous themselves in order to compensate, every time they strive not just to feel alive (which would be too paltry in comparison with their perceived indignities) but to become omnipotent, inviolable—or, on the other hand, simply collapse in the face of their exhaustion.

We also know that each of the power centers discussed were precisely great when those who represented them could face the perplexities of their past, when they could wrestle with those perplexities and entice people to be more fully present, discerning, and creative in response to them. In short, the power centers throughout history became great precisely at those precious points when they humbled themselves and became generously, inventively bold.

Given all of the above, we can draw the following plausible conclusions:

- *Polarization, the privileging of one reality to the wholesale exclusion of competing realities, is one of the chief scourges of humanity.* Polarization is responsible for countless deaths, degradations, and breakdowns, and its impact extends to all levels of humanity—personal, collective, psychological, and spiritual.

- *Cosmic insignificance, helplessness, and groundlessness are at the root of polarization.* This problem is illustrated by the large-scale suffering that leaders and cultures experience prior to their polarization. It is also illustrated by the lengths to which leaders and cultures will go to assert their significance—for example, through wars, decrees, religious symbols, and ethnic glorification. Whatever the form of the assertion, the repeated finding of this inquiry is that the assertion of significance must be cosmic in scope (grand and unassailable) in order to distinguish itself from its perceived adversary of cosmic unimportance. Although this view has its detractors,[8] the monumental work of such theorists as Eric Hoffer, Erich Fromm, Ernest Becker and, more recently, terror management theory shows convincingly that, whatever else may be at issue, the fear of insignificance (death or groundlessness) is a primary motive for human destructiveness—and that it is neglected at our peril (see

---

[8] The concept of deficient "self-esteem" as a basis of criminality, violence, and political extremism has recently come under intense criticism (e.g., Baumeister, Boden, & Smart, 1996; Haidt, 2012). However, this criticism itself must be subject to scrutiny. For example, most of this criticism stems from so-called objective studies which show that criminals have high—not low--self-esteem, and that the politically righteous are motivated chiefly by genetic assortment. Nonetheless, little of this research appears to derive from in-depth clinical investigations of criminal or extremist individuals, and therefore must be held in some doubt. It is a demonstrated fact, for example, that when people are asked about their mental health, they tend to respond more positively to paper-and-pencil tests than to trained clinical interviewers (see Shedler, Mayman, & Manis, 1993).

Mikulincer & Shaver, 2012 and Schneider, 2012   for reviews).

- *Cosmic insignificance arises from personal and collective trauma, ignorance, and fear, part of which appears inherent to mortal life.* Such damage prevents whole-bodied awareness of the awesome conditions of life.

- *The whole-bodied awareness of the awesome conditions of life means awareness of our smallness (e.g., fragility) as well as greatness (e.g., participation) in these conditions.* It also means the awareness of life's paradoxes, e.g., our apartness, humbleness that is simultaneously connectedness, wondrousness.

- *The acknowledgment of life's paradoxes begins with presence, which is the heightened "whole-bodied" awareness of the world around and within one.* There is reason to believe (e.g., Rank, 1929) that such whole-bodied awareness begins, although crudely and provisionally, at birth and can be carefully cultivated thereafter. Attachment issues are also pertinent to this cultivation, as the work of Shaver & Mikulincer (2012b) has convincingly demonstrated.

- *Presence is a precursor to awe, the humility and wonder—or sense of adventure—toward living. And awe is a scaffolding for wisdom.*

- *Wisdom is the "guidance system" for awe and leads to the fluidly centered life.* This is a life that is both pliable (fluid) and contained (centered) as context and circumstance demand.

- *The very power centers that become polarized also exhibit wisdom traditions.* These wisdom traditions (that include aspects of Taoism, Buddhism, and Confucianism in the East, Islam and Judaism in the Mid-East, and Greek Platonism, Roman Stoicism, Christianity, the Enlightenment, Romanticism, African American Gospel, and Transcendentalism in the West) draw on presence to the paradoxes, puzzles, and amazements of life. They are sometimes practical, sometimes political, and sometimes just simply personal and spiritual, but they are almost invariably agnostic in their outlook on the future. While they may certainly weigh in about issues of moral or practical import, they're explicitly tentative about the ultimate truth of those positions, and prefer to stress living over and above preaching the fruits of their discoveries. In sum, the wisdom traditions we have reviewed stress a fluid center of belief and action where constraint and pliability, humility and adventurousness are ever in play, ever in consideration, and ever in application to the world.

• *Revolutionary movements based largely on panic (trauma) tend to overreach and become polarized.* Revolutionary movements based largely on mindfulness and choice tend to set attainable goals and become inclusive. Examples of the latter include the many wisdom traditions previously discussed, along with their correlates in art, science, and politics.

• *Fear-based revolutionary movements (and individuals) tend to ignore the destruction in their wake. Awe-based revolutionary movements (and individuals) tend to acknowledge and redress the destruction in their wake.* Henry David Thoreau and Mahatma Gandhi, for example, called for nonviolent protest precisely to delimit the assaultive elements of their cause; George Washington withdrew from the opportunity to become a monarch explicitly to advocate for a freethinking republic. Stalin and Hitler, on the other hand, plowed through their totalizing visions heedless of the human cost.

To elaborate, what is needed now is something akin to an awe-based revolution. We need to explore awe-based revolutions (or potential revolutions) at every level of conflict, from that between liberal and conservative, fundamentalist and anarchist, worker and boss, teacher and student, and parent and child. While I and others have elaborated on the kernel of this idea elsewhere (e.g., Friedman, 2009; Lerner, 2000; Schneider, 2004, 2009), suffice it to say that person-to-person, professionally facilitated encounters among conflicting groups appear to be strikingly successful (e.g., Rogers, 1986). These encounters can include everything from intercultural sporting events to interethnic dialogues to commissions for restorative justice. The point here is to expand these opportunities, showcase them as model projects, and implement them wherever they are needed (which is just about everywhere!).

• *The strengthening of the sense of significance and the repair of substantive self-esteem are key building blocks for an awe-based reformation* (see, for example, Arndt, 2012 and Solomon, 2012 for overviews). The strengthening of self-esteem however, is not facilitated the way it has conventionally been portrayed. Simply heaping praise on children or bathing them in flowery descriptions about the world or their place in it will not, in the view of this study, substantively build their esteem. In fact, these bromides may not only harm their esteem because they will render kids ill-equipped to face their own and others' cruel realities, but they also may damage kids in a much subtler way: They may render kids ill-equipped to appreciate the depth and richness of an incomplete world, a world that beckons them to wonder, not only to tremble and withdraw. What this volume has demonstrated is that it is very difficult to know great joy unless one has had contact with great sorrow, and that exposure to anxieties can be as life affirming as limiting their impact. These paradoxes beg the following historically vexing yet imperative question: How and in what ways should kids be introduced to the fuller life, the curricula of unease right alongside those of support?

I believe that there is no definitive answer to this question. It is the creative challenge of every future generation of awe-based minds. However, one point that strikes clear and shines through the testimonies of this book is that *we need to be aware of the challenge.* We need to be aware that ignorance of life's paradoxes spells ignorance of life's flowering, and ignorance of life's flowering can only mean one thing: the squandering of a miracle.

References

Abrams, M.H. (1973). *Natural Supernaturalism: Tradition and Revolution in Romantic Literature.* New York, NY: Norton.

Adams, W.W. (2010). Basho's therapy for Narcissus: Nature as intimate other and transpersonal self. *Journal of Humanistic Psychology, 50,* 38–64.

Adorno, T., Frenkel-Brunswick, E., Levinson, D., & Sanford, R. (1950). *The authoritarian personality.* New York, NY: Harper & Row.

Ambrosio, F.J. (2009). *Philosophy, religion, and the meaning of life Parts I-III.* Chantilly, VA: The Teaching Company.

Angell, M. (2011, June 23). *The epidemic of mental illness: Why?* New York Review of Books, pp. 20–22.

Arndt, J. (2012). *A significant contributor to a meaningful cultural drama: Terror management research on the functions and implications of self-esteem.* In P. Shaver and M. Mikulincer (Eds.) *Meaning, mortality, and choice: The social psychology of existential concerns* (pp. 53–73). Washington, DC: American Psychological Association Press.

Armstrong, K. (2002). *Islam: A short history.* New York, NY: Modern Library.

Baeck, L. (1987). *The essence of Judaism.* New York, NY: Schocken.

Barks, C. (1995). *The essential Rumi* (C. Barks, Trans.). San Francisco, CA: HarperSanFrancisco.

Bauer, W. (1971). *Orthodoxy and heresy in earliest Christianity.* (R. Kraft, Trans.). Philadelphia: Fortress.

Baumeister, R.F., Boden, J.M., & Smart, L. (1996). Relation of threatened egotism to violence and aggression: The dark side of high self-esteem. *Psychological Review, 103,* 5–23.

Baumrind, D. (1971). Current patterns of parental authority. *Developmental Psychology Monograph, 4* (1), 1–103.

Beck (1976) *Cognitive therapy and the emotional disorders.*
    New York: New American Library.
Becker, E. (1967). *Beyond alienation: A philosophy of
    education.* New York, NY: George Braziller.
Becker, E. (1973). *The denial of death.* New York, NY: Free
    Press.
Becker, E. (1975) Escape from evil. New York: Free Press.
Berlin, I. (1999*). The roots of romanticism.* Princeton, NJ:
    Princeton University Press.
Berreby, D. (2011, March 6). *Names will hurt you.* New York
    Times Book Review.
Bishop, B. (2008). *The big sort: Why the clustering of like-
    minded America is tearing us apart.* New York, NY:
    Houghton Mifflin Harcourt.
Black, E. (2002/2012). *IBM and the holocaust: The strategic
    alliance between Nazi Germany and America's most
    powerful corporation.* Washington, DC: Dialog Press.
Blake, W. (1791/1988). *William Blake: Selected poetry.* New
    York, NY: Penguin.
Bly, R., Hillman, J., & Meade, M. (Eds.) (1992). *The rag and
    bone shop of the heart.* New York, NY: Harper
    Perennial.
Bonner, E.T. & Friedman, H.L. (2011). A conceptual
    clarification of the experience of awe: An interpretative
    phenomenological analysis. *The Humanistic
    Psychologist, 39,* 222–235.
Buckley, C. (2012). *The new student activism.* New York
    Times, January 22.
Campbell, J. (1948). *The hero with a thousand faces.* Princeton,
    NJ: Princeton University Press.
Campolo, T. (2010, January/February). *Married to Calvin: For
    better or worse.* Tikkun Magazine, 52–76.
Carson, C. (Ed.) (1998). *The autobiography of Martin Luther
    King Jr.* New York, NY: Warner Books.
Chan, W-T. (1963). *A sourcebook in Chinese philosophy.*
    Princeton, NJ: Princeton University Press.
Chang, I. (1997). *The rape of Nanking. The forgotten holocaust
    of World War II.* New York: Penguin.

Chang, J. & Halliday, J. (2005). *Mao: The unknown story*. New York, NY: Knopf.

Cleary, T. (1991). *The essential Tao* (T. Cleary, Trans.). San Francisco, CA: HarperSanFrancisco.

Conquest, R. (1991). *The great terror: A reassessment*. Oxford University Press, 1991.

Davies, P. (2009). *The French revolution*. Oxford, England: Oneworld Press.

Dillon, J.J. (2010). The primal vision: The psychological effects of the creation myth. *Journal of Humanistic Psychology, 50*, 495–513.

Doi, T. (1971). *The anatomy of human dependence*. Tokyo, Japan: Kodansha International.

Ehrman, B.D. (Lecturer) (2002). Lost Christianities: Christian scriptures and the battles over authentication. Chantilly, VA: The Teaching Co.

Eigen, M. (1993). *The psychotic core*. Northvale, NJ: Jason Aronson.

Eisler, R. (1987). *The chalice and the blade: Our history, our future*. New York, NY: Harper & Row.

Emerson, R.W. (1836/1992). *The selected writings of Ralph Waldo Emerson*. New York, NY: Modern Library.

Erikson, E. (1958). *Young man Luther: A study in psychoanalysis and history*. New York, NY: Norton.

Evans, R.J. (2008). *The third reich at war*. New York, NY: Penguin.

Federation of American Scientists (1998, February 23). Translation of Fatwa by Usama Bin Laden, retrieved from http://www.fas.org/irp/world/para/docs/980223-fatwa.htm

Ferguson, N. (2003). *Empire: The rise and demise of the British world order and the lessons for global power*. New York, NY: Basic Books.

Findlay, M.I. (1959). *The portable Greek historians: The essence of Herodotus, Thucydides, Xenophon, Polybus*. New York, NY: Viking.

Finkelstein, N.G. (2000). *The holocaust industry: Reflections on the exploitation of Jewish suffering*. London: Verso.

Firestone, R. W. & Catlett, J. (2009). *Beyond death anxiety: Achieving life-affirming death awareness.* New York: Springer.

Friedman, M. (2009). The outreach of dialogue. *Journal of Humanistic Psychology, 49,* 409–418.

Fromm, E. (1965). *Escape from freedom.* New York, NY: Holt, Rinehart, & Winston.

Garraty, J.A. & Gay, P. (1972). *The Columbia history of the world.* New York, NY: Harper & Row.

George, A. (1999). *The epic of Gilgamesh.* New York, NY: Penguin.

Goldberg, M. (2011, June 14). *Bachmann's unrivaled extremism.* The Daily Beast. (Retrieved from http://www.thedailybeast.com/articles/2011/06/14/miche le-bachmanns-unrivaled-extremism-gay-rights-to-religion.html

Gollwitzer, H. (1969). *Europe in the age of imperialism: 1880–1914.* New York: Harcourt, Brace, & World.

Greenberg, J., Koole, S. L., & Pyszczynski, T. (2004). *Handbook of experimental existential psychology.* Guilford Press.

Grottstein, J. (1990). The black hole as the basic psychotic experience: Some newer psychoanalytic and neuroscientific perspectives on psychosis. *Contemporary Psychoanalysis, 18,* 29–46.

Haidt, J. (2012). *The righteous mind.* New York, NY: Pantheon.

Hall, S. S. (2010). *Wisdom: From philosophy to neuroscience.* New York, NY: Knopf.

Heiden, K. (1925/1971). Introduction. In *Mein kampf* by A. Hitler. Boston, MA: Houghton Mifflin.

Herold, C. J. (2002). *The age of Napoleon.* New York, NY: Houghton Mifflin Harcourt.

Hitler, A. (1925/1971). *Mein kampf.* Boston. MA: Houghton Mifflin.

Hoffer, E. (1951). *The true believer.* New York, NY: Harper & Row.

Horner, F. J. (1948). *Case history of Japan.* New York, NY: Sheed & Ward.

Howard, R. (1977). *Mao Tse Tung and the Chinese people.* New York, NY: Monthly Review Press.

Jacobs, T. (2010). *The mind of a terrorist.* Miller-McCune, March-April, pp. 36-39.

James, W. (1907/1963). *Pragmatism and other essays.* New York. NY: Washington Square Press.

Jones, W.T. (1969). *Kant to Wittgenstein and Sartre: A history of Western philosophy.* New York: Harcourt, Brace, & World.

Kaplan, R.D. (2012). *The revenge of geography: What the map tells us about coming conflicts and the battle against fate.* New York, NY: Random House.

Kaufmann, W. (1975). *Existentialism from Dostoyevsky to Sartre.* New York: New American Library.

Kaufmann, W. (1968). *Nietzsche: Philosopher, psychologist, antichrist.* New York, NY: Vintage.

Keegan, J. (1993). *A history of warfare.* New York, NY: Vintage Books.

Keltner, D., & Haidt, J. (2003). Approaching awe, a moral, spiritual, and kinesthetic emotion. *Cognition and Emotion, 17,* 297–314.

Kierkegaard, S. (1849/1954). *Fear and trembling and the sickness unto death* (W. Lowrie, Trans.). Princeton, NJ: Princeton University Press. (Original works published in 1843 and 1849)

Kirschner, S. (1996). *The religious and romantic origins of psychoanalysis: Individuation and integration in post-Freudian theory.* Cambridge, UK: Cambridge University Press.

Klein, N. (2007). *The shock doctrine: The rise of disaster capitalism.* New York: Metropolitan Books.

Kohut, H. (1977). *The restoration of the self.* New York, NY: International Universities Press.

Kramer, J. & Alstad, D. (1993). *The guru papers: Masks of authoritarian power.* Berkeley, CA: Frog Books.

Kruglanski, A.W., Gelfand, M., & Gunaratna, R.(2012). Terrorism as means to an end: How political violence bestows significance. In P.R. Shaver & M. Mikulincer (Eds.) *Meaning, morality, and choice: The social*

psychology of existential concerns (pp. 203–212).
Washington, DC: American Psychological Association
Press.

Laing, R.D. (1967). *The politics of experience*. Middlesex,
England: Penguin.

Laing, R.D. (1969). *The divided self: A study in sanity and
madness*. Middlesex, England: Penguin.

Lao Tsu (1963). *Tao Te Ching* (D.C. Lau, Trans.). New York,
NY: Penguin.

Lerner, M. (2000). *Spirit matters: Global healing and the
wisdom of the soul*. Charlottesville, VA: Hampton Roads.

Lifton, R.J. (1986). *The nazi doctors*. New York, NY: Basic
Books.

Lila, M. (2001). *The reckless mind. Intellectuals in politics*.
New York, NY: New York Review of Books.

Maharaj, S.N. (1973). *I am that*. Durham, NC: Acorn Press.

Martin, R.L. (2009). *Opposable mind: Winning through
integrative thinking*. Cambridge, MA: Harvard Business
Review Press.

Maslow, A. (1968). *Toward a psychology of being*. New York,
NY: Van Nostrand.

Matrat, J. (1971/1901). *Robespierre, or the Tyranny of the
Majority* (Alan Kendall, Trans). New York, NY:
Charles Scribner's Sons.

May, R. (1991). *The cry for myth*. New York, NY: Norton.

McAdams, D.P. (2010). *George W. Bush and the redemptive
dream: A psychological portrait*. Oxford: Oxford
University Press.

McLetchie, S. (1983–1984). *Maximilien Robespierre: Master of
the Terror*, Vol. 15, pp. 1–15). Loyola University
Student Historical Journal.

Mendelowitz, E. (2008). *Ethics and Lao Tsu*. Colorado Springs,
CO: University of the Rockies Press.

Merker, D. (2009). The transference onto God. *International
Journal of Applied Psychoanalytic Studies, 6,* (2),
146–162.

Mikulincer, M. & Shaver, P. (2012). *Helplessness: A hidden
liability associated with failed defenses against
awareness of death*. In P. Shaver & M. Mikulincer

(Eds.) Meaning, mortality, and choice: The social psychology of existential concerns (pp. 37-53). Washington, DC: American Psychological Association Press.

Milbank, D., & VandeHei, J. (2003, May 17). May 1, 2003 Gallup poll. *The Washington Post.*

Milgram, S. (1962/2009). *Obedience to authority: An experimental view.* New York, NY: Harper Perennial Classics.

Miller, A. (1990). *The untouched key: Tracing childhood trauma in creativity and destructiveness.* New York, NY: Doubleday.

Miller, A. (2009). *Breaking down the wall of silence: The liberating experience of facing the painful truth.* New York, NY: Basic Books.

Mishra, P. (2010). *Staying power: Mao and the Maoists. The New Yorker,* December 20, pp. 124–130.

Nabokov, P. (1978). *Native American testimony.* New York, NY: Penguin.

Nichols, A. (2006). *Emerson, Thoreau, and the Transcendentalist movement* (Course guidebook, part 1). The Teaching Company.

Nietzsche, F. (1889/1982). *The portable Nietzsche.* New York: Penguin.

Occult history of the third reich (1991). The history channel. (Documentary). (D. Flitton, Dir.).

O'Connel Higgens, G. (1994). *Resilient adults: Overcoming a cruel past.* San Francisco, CA: Jossey-Bass.

Ortega y Gasset, J. (1932/1960). *The Revolt of the Masses.* New York, NY: Norton.

Otto, R. (1923). *The idea of the holy.* New York, NY: Oxford University Press.

Pagels, E. (1979). *The gnostic gospels.* New York, NY: Vintage Books.

Pascal, B. (1654/1991). Penses. In M. Friedman (Ed.), *The worlds of existentialism: A critical reader* (pp. 38–41). New Jersey: Humanities Press.

Pearsall, P. (2007). *Awe: The delights and dangers of our eleventh emotion.* Deerfield Beach, FL: Health Communications Inc.

Phillips, J. (2009). *Holy warriors: A modern history of the crusades.* New York, NY: Random House.

Plato (1984). *Great dialogues of Plato.* New York, NY: Mentor.

Prilleltensky, I. (2006). *Promoting well-being: Linking personal, organizational, and community change.* New York, NY: Wiley.

Pyszczynski, T., Solomon, S. & Greenberg, J. (2003). *"In the wake of 9/11: The psychology of terror."* American *Journal of Psychiatry* 160 *(5)*: 1019.doi:10.1176/ appi.ajp.160.5.1019.

Rank, O. (1929). *The trauma of birth.* New York, NY: Courier Dover.

Reston, J. (2005). *Dogs of God: Columbus, the Inquisition, and the defeat of the Moors.* New York, NY: Anchor Books.

Rogers, C.R. (1986). The rust workshop: A personal overview. *Journal of Humanistic Psychology, 26,* 23–45.

Rudd, M., Vohs, K.D., & Aaker, J. (2012). Awe expands people's perception of time, alters decision making, and enhances well-being. *Psychological Science* OnlineFirst. Published 8/10/12 as doi: 10.1177/ 0956797612438731.

Sandars, N.K. (1971). *Poems of heaven and hell from Mesopotamia.* New York, NY: Penguin.

Sandars, N.K. (1972). *The epic of Gilgamesh.* New York, NY: Penguin.

Schlesinger, A. (1986). *The cycles of American history.* New York, NY: Houghton Mifflin.

Schneider, K.J. (1999). *The paradoxical self: Toward an understanding of our contradictory nature.* Amherst, NY: Humanity Books.

Schneider, K.J. (2004). *Rediscovery of awe: Splendor, mystery, and the fluid center of life.* St. Paul, MN: Paragon House.

Schneider, K.J. (2009). *Awakening to awe: Personal stories of profound transformation.* Lanham, MD: Jason Aronson.

Schneider, K.J. (2012). The case of Allison: An existential-integrative inquiry into death anxiety, groundlessness, and the quest for meaning and awe. In P. Shaver and M. Mikulincer (Eds.) *Meaning, mortality, and choice: The social psychology of existential concerns* (pp. 339–352). Washington, DC: American Psychological Association.

Service, R. (2009). *A history of modern Russia: From tsarism to the twenty-first century.* Cambridge, MA: Harvard University Press.

Shaver, P.R. & Mikulincer, M. (Eds.) (2012a). *Meaning, mortality, and choice: The social psychology of existential concerns.* Washington, DC: American Psychological Association Press.

Shaver, P. & Mikulincer, M. (2012b). An attachment perspective on coping with existential concerns. In P. Shaver and M. Mikulincer (Eds.) *Meaning, mortality, and choice: The social psychology of existential concerns* (pp. 291–307). Washington, DC: American Psychological Association Press.

Shedler, J., Mayman, M., & Manis, M. (1993). The illusion of mental health. *American Psychologist, 48,* 1117–1131.

Simmonton, D.K. (1994). *Greatness.* New York, NY: Guilford.

Shirer, W. (1959). *The rise and fall of the third reich.* New York, NY: Simon & Schuster.

Smith, H. (1986). *The religions of man.* New York, NY: Harper & Row.

Smith, H. (1991). *The world's religions.* New York, NY: HarperCollins.

Snyder, T. (2010). *Bloodlands: Europe between Hitler and Stalin.* New York, NY: Basic Books.

Snyder, T. (2011, March 10). *Hitler vs. Stalin: Who killed more?* New York Review of Books.

Solomon, S. (2012). The social psychology of meaning, mortality, and choice: An integrative perspective on existential concerns. In P. Shaver and M. Mikulincer (Eds.) *Meaning, mortality, and choice: The social psychology of existential concerns* (pp. 401–417). Washington, DC: American Psychological Association Press.

Sternberg, R.J., Reznitskaya, A., & Jarvin, L. (2007). Teaching for wisdom: What matters is not just what students know but how they use it. *London Review of Education, 5,* 143–158.

Stolorow, R.D. (2011). *World, affectivity, trauma: Heidegger and Post-Cartesian psychoanalysis.* New York, NY: Routledge.

Suetonius (1979). *The twelve Caesars* (R. Graves, Trans.). New York, NY: Penguin. (Originally published in 96 C.E.).

Sunstein, C.R. (2011). *Going to extremes: How like minds unite and divide.* New York, NY: Oxford University Press.

The Economist. (2012, August 6). *The Turkish model: A hard act to follow.* Retrieved November 28, 2012 from http://www.economist.com/node/21525408.

Thoreau, H.D. (1854). *Walden.* New York, NY: Peebles Press International.

Tillich, P. (1952). *The courage to be.* New Haven, CT: Yale University Press.

Tillich, P. (1963a). *Systematic Theology: Volume I.* Chicago, IL: Chicago University Press.

Tillich, P. (Speaker). (1963b). *Romanticism* (Part 1). (CD recording T577 116, Paul Tillich Compact Disk Collection). Richmond, VA: Union PSCE.

Tolstoy, L. (1886/1960). *The death of Ivan Illych and other stories.* New York, NY: Signet.

Van Cappellen, P. & Saroglou, V. (2012). Awe activates religious and spiritual feelings and behavioral intentions. *Psychology of Religion and Spirituality, 4,* 223–236.

Van Wormer, K. (2002, October 11–13). *Bush and the dry drunk syndrome.* CounterPunch.

Walsh, S.J. (2011). *Healthy aging and wisdom: Moving throught the later years with grace.* San Francisco Medicine, 10-11.

Wansee Conference (1942). Retrieved from http://www.holocaust-history.org/short-essays/wannsee.shtml

Watts, A. (1994). *Talking Zen: Written and spoken by Alan Watts.* New York, NY: Weatherhill.

Weiner, E. (2010). *Americans: Undecided about God? New York Times* Sunday Review, December 10.

Weisberg, J. (2008). *The Bush tragedy.* New York, NY: Random House.

Whitman, W. (1855/1959). *Leaves of grass.* New York, NY: Penguin.

Woodward, B. (2006). *State of denial: Bush at war, part III.* New York, NY: Simon & Schuster.

Yalom, I. (1980). *Existential psychotherapy.* New York, NY: Basic Books.

Zinn, H. (2003). *A people's history of the United States: 1492–present.* New York, NY: Harper Perennial.

About the Author

KIRK J. SCHNEIDER, PhD, is a leading spokesperson for contemporary existential-humanistic psychology. Dr. Schneider is the recent past editor of the Journal of Humanistic Psychology (2005–2012), vice-president of the Existential-Humanistic Institute (EHI), and adjunct faculty at Saybrook University, Teachers College, Columbia University, and the California Institute of Integral Studies. A Fellow of the American Psychological Association (APA), Dr. Schneider has published over 100 articles and chapters and has authored or edited nine books (seven of which either have been or soon will be translated into Chinese). These books include *The Paradoxical Self, Horror and the Holy, The Psychology of Existence* (with Rollo May), *The Handbook of Humanistic Psychology* (with James Bugental and Fraser Pierson—now being updated for a second edition), *Rediscovery of Awe, Existential-Integrative Psychotherapy, Existential-Humanistic Therapy* (with Orah Krug—accompanying APA video also available), *Humanity's Dark Side: Evil, Destructive Experience, and Psychotherapy* (with Art Bohart, Barbara Held, and Ed Mendelowitz), and *Awakening to Awe.*

Index

CPSIA information can be obtained at www.ICGtesting.com
Printed in the USA
BVOW02s1959090914

366139BV00002B/6/P